Manifesting Possible Futures

towards a new genre of literature

JOHN C. WOODCOCK

iUniverse, Inc.
Bloomington

Manifesting Possible Futures
towards a new genre of literature

iUniverse books may be ordered through booksellers or by contacting:

iUniverse
1663 Liberty Drive
Bloomington, IN 47403
www.iuniverse.com
1-800-Authors (1-800-288-4677)

ISBN: 978-1-4759-6764-7 (sc)
ISBN: 978-1-4759-6765-4 (ebk)

Printed in the United States of America

iUniverse rev. date: 12/26/2012

Manifesting Possible Futures

CONTENTS

Permissions

Cover. *Sunset and Clouds*: Vera Kratochvil. http://www.publicdomainpictures.net/view-image.php?image=15811&picture=sunset-and-clouds.

Figure 1. *Tailor*: photo owned by author.

Figure 2. *Uncle Sam*: Public Domain.

Figure 3. *St. Matthew and the Angel*: Mikey Angels. http://en.wikipedia.org/wiki/File:Michelangelo_Merisi_da_Caravaggio_-_St_Matthew_and_the_Angel_-_WGA04127.jpg. (Wikimedia Commons).

Figure 4. *Medusa*: Nicolas Pioch. http://en.wikipedia.org/wiki/file:medusa_by_carvaggio.jpg. (Wikimedia Commons).

Figure 5. *New Pieta*: personal photo of sculpture by Fenwick Lawson. http://www.fenwicklawson.co.uk/. Permission granted.

Figure 6. *La Pieta (Michaelangelo)*: Stanislav Traykov. http://en.wikipedia.org/wiki/File:Michelangelo%27s_Pieta_5450_cropncleaned.jpg. (Wikimedia Commons).

Figure 7. *Lascaux Cave Painting*: Jack Versloot. http://en.wikipedia.org/wiki/File:Lascaux_II.jpg. (Wikimedia Commons).

Figure 8. *Angelus Novus*: Paul Klee. http://www.inicia.es/de/m_cabot/paul_klee.htm @ http://en.wikipedia.org/wiki/File:Klee,_Angelus_novus.png. (Wikimedia Commons).

Figure 9. *Tree*: by Author

Figure 10. *Waters Edge*: by Author

Figure 11. *Portrait.*: by Author.

PREFACE

Samuel John Woodcock was a tailor. He was man of small stature but obviously held a secret somewhere in that he also had a large family. He lived with his family in Chester, England—a town whose history stretches back to the Romans in 70 CE.

S. J. Woodcock carried on his trade in a little room at the back of their cramped, modestly appointed flat.

His customers were always satisfied with his handiwork and often marvelled at the dextrous manner in which their usual lumps and bumps were masterfully transformed into graceful curves or intriguing interstices. His professional reputation was thus assured and he and his family prospered as long as his wife kept a firm and guiding hand on their daily expenses.

But S. J. Woodcock held another secret, one that belonged to the tiny alcove hidden behind a curtain in the recess at the back of his work space. There was nothing there that encouraged speculation: a small rosewood desk; an upright chair made from dark cherry wood, with no cushions; a lamp that cast a pale light over some stray papers. There was also a set of needles and thread, his tools of trade, at the side of the desk, along with a tape measure. And of course, a very large pair of Pinking shears laid half-open on top of pieces of paper that were used to cut various patterns. A small cot, with a pillow, and a thin blanket lay against the opposite wall.

The only curiosity left to his family concerning this alcove was that the tailor never used it to do his regular work. When asked, he would simply say, "That's where I do my thinking, luv" and the matter would drop.

What nobody knew was that the little tailor was an adept. He had been trained as an *Iatromantis*—a spiritual practice of incubation that began at least with Parmenides. [1] In this practice lay S. J. Woodcock's true calling and mastery. His work as a tailor had achieved a level of refinement that few knew about. He knew how to go to the cot, lie down, and simply surrender to what would then come to him. He did have one "device" that helped him get there. He could conjure up a very stable image of his Pinking shears and use them to pierce a hole in the garment of time. Whenever he did this act, a pungent odour would fill his nostrils and he would then know that he had "reached" the other side.

---

[1]   For a fuller, masterful, exposition of this ancient practice see: (Kingsley, 2001)

In this way he had succeeded in connecting with his great grandson whose name was also John:

SJ: John, John, can you hear me, lad. I am with you now.

J: Yes Grandfather, I can smell the pungency. You've pierced through.

SJ: What do you need today?

J: Thank you for coming again. I have so much to do. It's all pressing on me quite hard.

SJ: Well, lad, don't press too hard, you will burn the cloth, and we can't have that, can we?

J: Dreams, memories, events from my childhood, theory, speculation, intuitions, possible futures, inner and outer facts, are all coming down on me like shards, and I am getting a bit lost in the chaos.

SJ: Steady on steady on lad. I told you I am here for you. Relax. Take a breath of that pungent odour. Breathe it in slowly. Yes, you are coming more into focus now. Good! Now we can begin.

J: Where shall we start?

SJ: It doesn't matter. Just give me some cloth. What did you call it—shard! Yes, that memory will do. Oh, and most certainly that current event in your life can go here. That one is good—a philosophical speculation, yes, very good. Hmm, Hmm, Oh yes, I like that. Inner becomes outer, outer goes inside with a little stitch here, a tuck there. Did you know lad that outer becomes inner through a tuck that turns the thing entirely inside out and upside down. What was on the outside with us looking at it from the outside now becomes the inside with us inside it? They are really the same thing, lad, the trick lies in the tuck. Future, past—Hah! A stitch in time no more. Fold the stitch and what do you have? *Simultaneity*! Are you following my pattern here lad?

J: I am beginning to, Grandfather. One has to give up so much to follow your threads here.

SJ: *Selvege*, lad! Think of the effort required to keep the warp and weft in place. Centuries, millennia! All we are doing is loosening it a bit so we can breathe. Yes breathe, lad. Now listen to me closely here. It's all about letting go, surrender, remember? *Iatromantis*! I taught the practice to you. Well, it is done! What do you think? Do you like it? I serged the edges again and you won't see any seams.

J: Grandfather, as I said before, I don't know what to make of this garment you have made for me, like all the others. I think we will have to wait to see what others think, don't you. They will have to judge whether it is a seamless garment or not. How many can even judge such a garment that weaves together so many different qualities of time? But, Grandfather, before you go, I have been playing with a name for this garment of ours, would you like to hear . . . ?

SJ: Now, now, lad, it's a little too soon for that. Just wear it for now. Others may come to name it down the seam. I must go now.

Remember, lad, your pen is the needle and thread. Mind is the precious cloth. Let go, let go, your hands will do the seam ripping and the stitching.

Write to me, John, no, write FOR me, for us . . .

FOUR CONDITIONS

In July 2008, my wife Anita and I visited the *2008 Biennale of Sydney*, a gathering of events and artists to celebrate the theme, *Revolutions—Forms that Turn*. We took a ferry to Cockatoo Island, lying low in the Sydney Harbour, an aging has-been of past human endeavours. There were relics of a ship yard as well as convict cells and abandoned buildings. As we stepped off the boat, I was immediately drawn to a low hole in the sheer granite wall that confronted us. We wandered through a tunnel cut into the cliff while eerie music played along with us. We emerged, finding huge buildings big enough to construct ships but now mostly empty caverns. The scale of the work that once took place there was magnificent. Hooks capable of lifting hundreds of tons were now suspended uselessly in space; engines and gears equally huge, lay idle. And in amongst these Titans of the past, artists had placed their works as part of the festival.

We ambled our way to a large broken building that housed the works of one Mike Parr. It was well out of the way for a good reason. Only those who can "abandon all hope" should enter this gate. Here is what the program guide said about Parr's work as an artist:

> *In the derelict and dilapidated building of the former sailors'*
> *quarters and naval 'academy' on Cockatoo Island, Mike Parr*
> *theatrically stages a presentation of 17 of his most daring*
> *and demanding performances since he began exploring the*
> *field in 1971 to test the emotional and physical limits of the*
> *human body. This dramatic installation on Cockatoo Island,*
> *titled 'MIRROR/ARSE', presents filmic documentation of his*
> *performance works in a deliberately episodic and disconnected*

1

> *way, as the viewer enters into corridors and rooms with peeling walls, collapsed ceilings, undisturbed rubbish and pools of water. Just as the viewer's encounter with the architecture of the space is traumatic, so do Parr's works explore trauma and subjectivity. Parr, in the great Expressionist tradition, denounces and is outraged by the brutality of the world we live in. He is revolted by it, and creates poignant artworks where the viewer is confronted with revolting situations, hopefully achieving turns that form consciousness.*

That's what the program said and we actually saw videos of the artist subjecting his own body to various forms of mutilation or showing us equally graphic acts of horror. Just one example: he allowed someone to stitch his face into a contorted mask of horror to register his "artistic response" to the treatment of illegal immigrants here in Australia. He had no anaesthetic and we were spared none of the pain as the sutures were sewn into his face and pulled tight.

Having read the program description and also seen the exhibit, I was startled by the choice of the word "poignant" to describe his work. The word springs from a root *peuk* which does not mean what I felt like doing and what the artist actually did in one display. The root is an image of pricking, which certainly conveys pain, and to be poignant is to be piercingly incisive, as well as skilfully to the point.

However, this word also carries a meaning of being moved, touched by the skilful astute application of pain. The sponsors no doubt had in mind that Parr's work, graphic as it is would have the effect of revolution on the audience, i.e. move us, or turn us in some way by a skilful application of pain. But this emphatically did not happen, at least to me. Where I was supposed to be moved, I was instead frozen, my psyche barely able to function at all beyond registering the stark horror of what he was doing, what he was portraying. I could not imagine at all, let alone imagine into the acts of horror, perceiving within their underlying logical structure, some seed of a new possibility. My psyche was immobilized by this art, not moved at all into new fresh channels of thinking or perceiving. The shock of this art I suspect induces either *reactions* (dissociating, numbing etc.) or *fascination*. I am equally sure that there were some observers, who were willing to see the world the same way that Parr does—as a primary seat of brutality and horror, in which the human body is merely a lump of meat.

This episode contains all that I want to say in my book. It illustrates the necessary conditions for a transformation in reality or, to put it another way, a simultaneous transformation in the form of consciousness and world. We may tentatively articulate these conditions as follows:

1. The individual effort of participation with an aspect of *possible* futures;
2. The enactment, by this individual, of his or her participation, thereby becoming a *mouthpiece* of this future;
3. The willingness on the part of others to make a move towards "seeing" (conceiving) the world the same way the individual does;
4. The gradual congealing of that conception into the way the world is perceived, the world thus becoming, over time, "that way", resulting in cultural forms that give expression to and strengthen that new reality.

When these conditions are met then we, as psychological beings, and the real world in which we live, transform. We end up living in that world. It becomes really so!

These four conditions are succinctly outlined and examined in the following passage by Owen Barfield [2]

> *Imagination is not, as some poets have thought, simply synonymous with good. It may be either good or evil. As long as art remained primarily mimetic, the evil which imagination could do was limited by nature . . . [b]ut . . . when the fact of the directionally creator relation is beginning to break through into consciousness, both the good and evil latent in the working of imagination begin to appear unlimited . . . . we could very*

---

[2] (Barfield, 1957, pp. 145-146)

well move forward into a chaotically empty or fantastically hideous world . . . .

We should remember this, when appraising the aberrations of the formally representational arts . . . . in so far as they are genuine, they are genuine because the artist has in some way experienced the world he represents. And in so far as they are appreciated, they are appreciated by those who themselves are willing to make a move towards seeing the world in that way and, ultimately therefore, seeing that kind of world. We should remember this, when we see pictures of a dog with six legs emerging from a vegetable marrow or a woman with a motor-bicycle substituted for her left breast.

TARNING AS
THE PROCESS OF MANIFESTING
POSSIBLE FUTURES

The four conditions that must be met for the manifestation of a possible future are condensed in the concept of tarning—a concept coined by Owen Barfield who adapted the word from the German *tarnung*: "The word *Tarnung* was, I believe, extensively used under the heel of the Nazi tyranny in Germany for the precautionary practice of hiding one meaning in another." [3]

Barfield needed this concept to name the process of advancing new meaning in culture through language. Dictionaries are an expression of congealed meanings, or norms, in language but these norms do change over time, as etymology teaches us. The concept of tarning gives us a means to examine these changes, through a microscope, as it were.

When a possible future is pressing forward into consciousness, as a new meaning, then the human participant in effect has something new to say but this new meaning must be said through already established words (dictionary meanings). It must be this way because speaking new meaning in a totally new word would be unintelligible to others. There must be some *communication* as well as *expression*, in order for others to grasp the new meaning that is suggested through the use of the old word. An example

---

[3]   (Barfield, 1977, p. 55 ff)

of tarning that borders on the unintelligible, i.e., is mostly expressive and least communicative is Lewis Carroll's *Jabberwocky*: [4]

> *'Twas brillig, and the slithy toves*
> *Did gyre and gimble in the wabe:*
> *All mimsy were the borogoves,*
> *And the mome raths outgrabe.*

In this case there does appear to be some tarning in which new meaning is meant through the use of established words, which are, however, considerably "distorted", e.g. "slimy" becoming "slithy" etc. But when I read this famous passage I do at least get strange images of swamps and weird dancing.

Tarning is a process in which: [5]

> *Every man, certainly every original man, has something new to say, something new to mean. Yet if he wants to express that meaning (and it may be that it is only when he tries to express it, that he knows what he means) he must use language—a vehicle which presupposes that he must either mean what was meant before or talk nonsense!*

> *If therefore he would say anything really new, if that which was hitherto unconscious is to become conscious, he must resort to tarning. He must talk what is nonsense on the face of it, but in such a way that the recipient may have the new meaning suggested to him. This is the true importance of metaphor.*

In other words, Barfield has given us a concept so that we can begin to think the process of a possible future emerging into consciousness through individual participation, and thence into metaphorical language which may be discerned as such by others. The new meaning thus begins its "descent" into manifestation and finally, "world" (see the four conditions cited above).

---

4   (Carroll, 2012)

5   Ibid, p. 68

Barfield gives a particularly compelling example of tarning in his beautiful "historical imagination" of Jesus' parable of the Sower and its effect on his disciples. The nascent meaning of the Logos appearing "in earthly soil", i.e., in the hearts and minds of his listeners (at least for those who hath ears) was spoken *through* the well-established external meaning of sowing in the earth. [6]

Tarning, then, is a concept that neatly conveys the four conditions for the manifestation of possible futures, beginning with a nascent appearance within an individual who participates in its becoming. The individual then expresses/communicates to those others who "hath ears to hear". The listeners (who hath ears) must necessarily have the same seed of new meaning within them, too, i.e., the same possible future must be approaching them as well. Further manifestation than occurs as the new meaning sinks into habitual use, becoming in turn a perception or "world"—actuality!

A critical emphasis is needed here in discussing Barfield's concept of tarning: "If therefore he would say anything really new, if that which was hitherto unconscious is to become conscious, he must resort to tarning". This crucial aspect of tarning points to the enormous creative effort by the individual to "find the right words" that will no longer mean what they usually mean but instead will mean the new meaning, which cannot be said explicitly, but can only be suggested. This is the essence of tarning and the phenomenology of manifesting possible futures.

Barfield reminds us of the intimate and pervasive connection between tarning and language: [7]

> *Everywhere in language we seem to find that the process of tarning, or something very like it is or has been at work. We seem to owe all these tropes and metaphors embedded in language to the fact that somebody at some time had the wit to say one thing and mean another, and that somebody else had*

---

[6]   (Barfield, 1957, p. 178 ff)

[7]   (Barfield, 1977, p. 57)

the wit to tumble to the new meaning, to detect the bouquet of a new wine emanating from the old bottle.

Tracing back from a given congealed cultural form, or established meaning, or perceived aspect of the real world (Condition 4), to the individual effort (Condition 1) is difficult but not impossible, Shakespeare being an outstanding example of a known individual who infused our entire culture with 1700 fresh words as well as many new phrases. If we succeed in doing so, we can get a microscopic glimpse of the "primal stuff", in the form of thinking or image that the individual participated, on the way to bringing the transformed matter into the world (Conditions 1 and 2).

There are some modern examples where it is possible to not only trace back to the individual effort but to demonstrate all four conditions still at work in shaping reality today. These examples also demonstrate different scales in which the world and consciousness can transform.

SOME EXAMPLES OF TARNING

Mandelbrot and the Fractal

If you look up *fragment* in the America Heritage Dictionary, you can go to the "root" *bhreg*, which is said to be the original sound-meaning from which a host of cognates spring. The root carries an image of breaking and one of the cognates mentioned is *fractal*. To the uninformed reader this word, with its collective meaning of a geometrical shape in which self-similar patterns are found across scale, simply belongs with all its sibling words as if for all time. Yet its birth as a word can be traced to a specific time and to a specific individual: [8]

> *One wintry afternoon in 1975, aware of the parallel currents emerging in physics, preparing his first major work for publication in book form, Mandelbrot decided he needed a new name for his shapes, his dimensions, and his geometry. His son was home from school, and Mandelbrot found himself thumbing through the boy's Latin dictionary. He came across the Latin* fractus, *from the verb* frangere, *to break. The resonance of the main English cognates—fracture and fraction—seemed appropriate. Mandelbrot created the word . . . fractal.*

Such a tiny moment: two known words *fracture* and *fragment* are joined to form a new word: *fractal*. This new word facilitated new meaning into the world. As Gleick reports, Mandelbrot had spent twenty years extending his perception into an aspect of reality (its "regular-irregularity") for which

---

[8]   (Gleick, 1997, p. 98)

he yet had no word. He had to invent it to convey his new perception. Now the word and its meaning are widely accepted.

Those who follow Mandelbrot's pioneering work can like-wise extend their perceptions into reality through the agency of the concept he brought forward. Although the *fractal nature* of the world has not yet gained universal acceptance, (in the way that atoms have for example, or gravity, or geometric space), it now is in the public market of competing meanings, along with other conceptions of nature that are appearing. [9]

Bernays And Public Relations

This is not a harmless process as we can see in the example of Edward Bernays. Ideas were swirling around the West during and after the First World War. Freud had discovered the unconscious and conceived it as a vessel of hidden desires that threaten the stability of the ego that seeks to conform to its environment. These desires are dangerous, animal-like, requiring defences. He later famously wrote *Civilization and its Discontents* in which he portrays civilization as the only bulwark against the Visigoth-like desires of the unconscious. Since these desires should never be released, civilized people are always in a state of necessary discontent. [10] Another idea sharpened into focus during the war and concerned the deliberate manipulation of "the masses" for purposes of war. Propaganda was taken up by governments to control public opinion in order to further its own cause. These two ideas, fermenting independently in the pool of available ideas simply needed a fertile imagination to unite in what we may someday describe as an "unholy marriage". This fertile imagination belonged to Edward Bernays who was working for the American Government as a press agent during the war. His slogan: *Make the World safe for Democracy* became a major player in the propaganda effort. He was also the nephew of Sigmund Freud.

---

[9]   (Rayner, 2010)
[10]   (Freud, 1961)

After the war Bernays asked a simple question: Is it possible to manipulate the masses for purposes of *peace*? The two ideas flowed together into one and the field of Public Relations was born. Edward Bernays brought the ideas together under this new concept. His goal was "the conscious and intelligent manipulation of the organized habits and opinions of the masses . . ." His methodology was to stimulate unconscious desires in people and then extinguish those desires in a commercial product. The effect of this method is to make people into consuming, docile "happiness machines" while the "few" in power pursue their own political and economic ends. [11]

I felt the full extent of his effects on our culture when I was in New York in 2004. My wife and I were on the street near Times Square when a young man invited us to the *David Letterman Show*. We decided to go and witness this "archbishop of the inconsequential". We were not disappointed. In an advertising segment, he paired the horrors of Iraq with a product called *Atomic Popcorn*. The subliminal message is:

All your unconscious fears and anxieties can safely be extinguished in a bag of light fluffy candy whose explosion (pop!) cannot possibly hurt you.

Public Relations at its finest!

We can witness the enormous cultural influence that Edward Bernays' ideas have today. There are many eloquent critics who point out the excesses of misinformation that shape public opinion today but the phenomenon seems unstoppable. Any criticism is merely twisted into another aspect of the propaganda. As early as 1933, Bernays caught wind of the possibility of his ideas being taken up in a way that was less than wholesome. Goebbels, supreme architect of Nazi propaganda, had used Bernays' book *Crystallizing Public Opinion* as a basis for his own destructive campaign against the Jews of Germany. Bernays was shocked. [12] I wonder today if he would be proud or horrified at the level of sophistication attained by the Public Relations Industry and its role in shaping the Iraq War, for

---

[11] (Bernays, 1928, p. 9)

[12] (Bernays, 1965)

example. The Public Relations industry has become so bold, so confident of its own abilities, that it does not need to hide or disguise its theories, manipulations etc. I remember the movie in which a Hollywood director was hired by the CIA to "invent" a completely fictitious war that existed only on the TV sets of millions of Americans. It was brilliantly conceived and carried out. [13]

Whatever we may think of Public Relations and its determinative force in the world today, its possibility began in the imagination of one individual who, like Mandelbrot, accepted the union of two disparate ideas and chose to incarnate that union in a new concept, bringing forward new meaning and shaping the world accordingly.

As these and other examples show, for the first time in the history of our species we are participating in the formation of possible futures on an unprecedented scale. In former times, only individual geniuses like Shakespeare rose to the level of participation in reality's underlying logic and its self-transformation. Today we seem to be in a collective uproar of more or less conscious participation in the transformation of consciousness and reality as a multitude of art forms burst into the bewilderingly complex market of meanings. More and more individuals show a willingness to encounter the spontaneous weavings of the soul and then to make choices to incarnate this or that image of possible futures. We only need to glance at the plethora of "New Age" books in which the author claims that he or she is channelling the voices(s) of the spirit which is informing them and us of an imminent future reality.

Baljeu and Downloading Spirit

To give a taste of such literature I will here reproduce a portion of the Foreword I wrote to a remarkable book which describes both the author's participation with a possible future, and her attempt to bring forward a theory of a new reality: [14]

---

[13] *Wag the Dog* (1997) starring Dustin Hoffman and Robert de Niro.

[14] (Baljeu, 2012)

Janet gives us an account of how she received the messages that comprises Chapters 1-5:

"The tall golden being I call Esau is my personal connection with the consciousness of Abraham. He is my teacher. He stands by me through the night to translate into my brain any messages from Abraham. As he told me in 2005:

"I come in dreams. Dreams are the way you understand best."

In other words, Janet received this stream of ideas as one would receive a dream. She has not yet worked them into reflective brain-thinking, the kind of effort that leads to theory, which can then be scrutinised. We must wait for Chapter Six for that . . . .

When I began reading the first five chapters, I quickly became submerged in the chaotic flow of ideas. As much as I wanted to attach to one idea and dwell on it, I was quickly swept away by another. Whereas I usually think of myself as possessing my own thoughts which are "inside" me, I found that now I was now "inside" thoughts that had their own life and were decidedly not my possession. At times I felt I was drowning. But I didn't. I came through, as Janet must have come through her dream-like encounters with Esau-Abraham . . .

Baljeu's book is a striking example of the process of tarning where: [15]

> *One of the beings coming through called himself Mischka. He kept telling me to extrapolate. Over the next three years I did so much extrapolating I often felt I'd never finish. I seemed to be going in circles, pacing the floor, crying with frustration, learning, reading, researching, making notes, drafts. I was obsessive, being driven by I knew not what. At times, I was exhausted and overwhelmed. Then finally I began to understand. It was a moment of epiphany. The writing began.*

---

[15] Ibid: p. 17.

Baljeu's own explanation of the process of *extrapolation* is this: [16]

> *Extrapolation for me is like automatic writing or as Eugene O'Neil calls it a 'stream of consciousness'. In computer language, it's streaming information through your computer which is being generated from another vibrational source. It can only be done if your computer is logged on and the interfaces active. Information comes into my consciousness.*

We can see here that a new meaning is manifesting but can only be said through the established word "extrapolate" whose dictionary meaning is quite different from the nascent one emerging through Baljeu's participation.

While it is not clear how many people are willing to see the world in the way Mike Parr or Janet Baljeu does, it does seem clear that the individual efforts of Mandelbrot and Bernays have found many more people "willing to see the world the same way". Whether these possible futures will last, or prevail, remains to be seen but they all do demonstrate the four conditions that need to be met for the manifestation of any possible future.

There is a much more powerful and complex example of this simultaneous process of transformation of consciousness and the form of the world. It is also an example demonstrating how the manifestation of a possible future can actually prevail and become a reality worldwide. In this next example we will see how the four conditions required for transformation of reality have indeed been satisfied, leading to cultural forms that reflect and strengthen this "new world" through the force of habit. I say "new world" in quotes to emphasise that our current situation is still fluid, even chaotic, and no possible future has stabilized into universal reality as yet. We are still very much "in between", a time equally of great peril and opportunity.

---

[16]   Ibid: p. 105.

C. G. Jung and the Jungian Unconscious

In 2009 a truly remarkable book was published: *The Red Book*, by C. G. Jung. [17] This long-awaited book shows the psychological process Jung underwent and endured over several years, culminating in the Jungian conception of the unconscious. He called this period of his life his confrontation with the unconscious. [18] However, *The Red Book* shows much more than the development of a conscious concept. It also shows us how a possible future manifests through the efforts and participation of one individual, Jung.

In Shamdasani's Introduction to *The Red Book*, he describes the beginnings of Jung's decades-long involvement (1912-1959) with *The Red Book* and the *Black Books* that preceded it: [19]

> *Up to this point, Jung had been an active thinker and had been averse to fantasy: 'as a form of thinking I held it to be impure, a sort of incestuous intercourse, thoroughly immoral from an intellectual viewpoint'. He now turned to analyse his fantasies . . .*
>
> *Jung picked up the brown notebook which he had set aside in 1902, and began writing in it . . . it occurred to him that he could write down his reflections in a sequence. He was "writing autobiographical material but not as an autobiography."*

Jung called his activity an experiment, an intentional procedure in which he "switched off consciousness", deliberately "evoking a fantasy in a waking state, and then entering it as into a drama". His aim was "to allow psychic contents to appear spontaneously. He recalled that beneath the threshold of consciousness, everything was animated. At times it was as if he heard something. At other times, he realized he was whispering to himself".

---

[17]   (Jung, 2009)

[18]   (Jung, 1963, p. 170ff)

[19]   All the following quotes from Shamdasani appear in the Introduction to *The Red Book*: pp. 193-221.

Shamadasani reports Jung's uncertainty during this period (1913) concerning the meaning and significance of his undertaking. This uncertainty lasted throughout his life, leading to much ambivalence concerning its publication. As late as 1959, two years before his death, Jung once again approached *Liber Novus* (what we also know as *The Red Book*) in order to complete it but broke off mid-sentence. He had previously suggested that "it and the *Black Books* be given to the library of the University of Basel with a restriction of 50 years, 80 years, or longer . . ."

Perhaps the most succinct expression of Jung's uncertainty concerning the nature of *The Red Book*, or his activities recorded therein appears in dialogue form in his second *Black Book*. A voice informs him unambiguously that what he is doing is art—a claim that he vigorously disputes, making the counter-claim that what he is doing is nature. Only a portion of the long dialogue seems to be available at this time (2012) but has been source of serious discussion and speculation subsequently within the Jungian community. [20]

Shamdasani describes the overall content of *The Red Book* as a series of active imaginations together with Jung's attempt to understand their significance. He further describes the overall theme of the book as how "Jung regains his soul and overcomes the contemporary malaise of spiritual alienation". This is achieved through the "rebirth of a new image of God in his soul and developing a new worldview in the form of a psychological and theological cosmology".

Shamdasani's understanding of the content and theme of *The Red Book* finds resonance with Jung's own words as recorded in his well-known letter to Sir Herbert Read in 1960 in which he speaks of the "great Dream" and identifies it with "the future and the picture of the new world". [21]

Lockhart comments that the emphasis here is not on "the ego's predicting the future—using dreams for power—but on man's conscious reflection and eros involvement in responding to the images bearing the incipient

---

[20] (Hillman, 1981), (Lockhart, 1987), (Giegerich, 2010).

[21] (Jung, 1975, p. 586)

future in such a way as to participate *with* God in the birth of the manifest future". [22]

From this brief overview of Jung's conscious intentions in writing *The Red Book* we can see that Jung was actively involved in a psychological process that demanded *both* his understanding and participation in it. His *understanding*, as well as that of subsequent commentators, is of the birth within himself of a new reality, a birth which as he later says was "the material that burst forth from the unconscious, and at first swamped me. It was the *prima materia* for a lifetime's work". [23]

Shamdasani shows how Jung indeed went on to develop and refine his understanding, producing a plethora of fresh and lasting contributions to our culture. [24]

In this way we can see a *semantic continuity* between the content in *The Red Book* and Jung's subsequent life-long work as a psychologist of the soul. It appears that all subsequent auditors accept Jung's own position that the meaning of *The Red Book* is that of "*prima materia* for a lifetime's work". That is to say, we can successfully examine *The Red Book* to find the origin of Jung's later, more fully developed thought. In this way the understanding of future scholars or members of the Jungian community simply imitates Jung's own ideas about the meaning of *The Red Book* carrying them further into manifestation (Conditions 3 and 4), without questioning Jung's own understanding of the meaning of his activities recorded in *The Red Book*. [25]

A possible future has definitely manifested and flourished since Jung's time. We could call it the Jungian worldview which has touched the

---

[22] (Lockhart, 1987, p. 115)

[23] (Jung, 1963, p. 199)

[24] (Jung, 2009, p. 207)

[25] The outstanding exception is the work of Wolfgang Giegerich who is to date the only Jungian theoretician to analyse *The Red Book* more deeply than merely accepting Jung's position about the meaning of the text. The reader may find Giegerich's analysis in the following works: (Giegerich, 2010), (Giegerich, 2007a), (Giegerich, 2003), (Giegerich, 2012).

lives of many and produced a profusion of secondary literature and other cultural forms that simply would not have been possible without Jung's seminal ideas, all of which originates, as he says, in *The Red Book*.

The Jungian worldview holds that, within us, i.e., "in the unconscious", there may be found those precious soul qualities that modern life longs for, since the end of the metaphysical world, or, as Barfield says, the Aristotelian "mindscape": [26]

> *Our contemporary "mindscape" dates back roughly to the Scientific revolution . . . It was preceded by a very different mindscape, which had endured from some time in the first millennium BC to about the seventeenth century AD; and which I will call "Aristotelianism" . . . this earlier mindscape was one which assumed an intercommunion between man (the microcosm) and nature (the macrocosm) . . .*

These soul qualities include interconnectedness, wisdom, and divinity in nature (imaginal depth), immediacy of appearance, numinosity, and autonomy of an intelligent *other-as-subject*—all those qualities that have disappeared from modern existence, as so many poets, artists, and philosophers have articulated, and as so many ordinary people sense today.

Within the Jungian community and to some extent beyond, particularly in the relatively new discipline of eco-psychology, Jung's historically new view of human beings (as carrying within themselves those soul qualities that once invested the world with meaning) has been taken up by others who "agreed" to see things the same way as Jung, and therefore, finally, to see the world that way: [27]

> *(Jung's) main argument is that what we have lost, we have to find again. Even in this statement he concedes that the psychic connection to the cosmos has "sunk into the unconscious." That is why in dreams, he believes, we can still experience the ancient*

---

[26]   (Barfield, 1977, p. 217)

[27]   (Tacey, 2010)

> *mystical at-one-ment with nature that is lost to our rational or*
> *waking mind.*

In this way, Jung's concept of the unconscious has entered the public market of meanings, competing, like the fractal, public relations, and many New Age messages, in the formation of a future reality the final form of which is as yet not known.

VOLUNTARY PURPOSE AND SPONTANEOUS IMPULSE

It is clear that, in each of these modern examples, a new concept or worldview has been produced to some degree through the creative efforts of individuals. And it is equally clear that others have to some degree agreed to see the world that way and, finally to see that kind of world (Conditions 1-4). Whether and to what degree they each involve tarning, i.e., the process of possible futures *emerging from the unconscious* and becoming manifest requires a still more microscopic examination. Tarning is "the concept of saying one thing and meaning another"—symbols, metaphors, and similes being the prime carriers of such speech. [28]

Barfield's example of the parables of Jesus demonstrates tarning at work in that Jesus had to say "A" in order to mean "B". In so doing, "B" *could* manifest through "A". There is no other way for this manifestation to happen. In so speaking, Jesus was not merely espousing a new worldview, one that he had consciously thought up and decided to deliver cryptically to his disciples. [29] Rather he and his disciples were participating in the emergence of a possible future emerging from "within" or spirit. This episode of tarning involved the momentous, historically new, and previously un-heard of, transformation of *interiority* (logos) from nature to man. There was no human "unconscious" previous to that time—"within-ness" or interiority was the interiority of nature, not the interiority of human

---

[28] (Barfield, 1977, p. 55)

[29] As Barfield says . . . *and it may be that it is only when he tries to express it, that he knows what he means.* See his quote on *tarning* above.

beings. In the parables we can see the very process of transfer of interiority out of nature to man: [30]

> *The parable, then, was about the sowing of the world, the Logos, in earthly soil. It was an attempt to awaken his hearers to this realization that this seed was within their own hearts and minds, and no longer in nature or anywhere without.*

Barfield goes on to remind us that "transition" is a "misleading word for the violent change in the whole direction of human consciousness which, in the last resort, this must involve". The violence done to Jesus is of course well-known and even raised to the highest value but elsewhere Barfield gives us a stark picture of this "violent change", in reference to the possible abandonment of *our* current reality (what he and many others call Cartesianism) in favour of a new reality (as yet, of course, unknown): [31]

> *It might be thought that . . . such a change could take place without any great upheaval. After all even in our Cartesian world quite a number of people seem to hold theories about the relation between man and nature which are incompatible with an absolute gulf between mind and matter . . . but any forecast based on such considerations . . . overlooks the extent to which Cartesianism has progressed from conscious to unconscious or "subliminal" conviction. "Materialism" . . . means, not any materialistic philosophy . . . but a mental habit of taking for granted, for all practical purposes and most theoretical ones, that the human psyche is intrinsically "alienated" from nature . . . a habit so inveterate as to have entered into the meanings of a great many common words and thus to have been accepted as common sense itself. Materialism in this sense is not, for instance, incompatible with deep religious conviction.*

If tarning is at work then, we may expect to find, as well as the four conditions that I proposed above (which appear in Barfield's quote here above), signs of resistance even in the "hearers", i.e., those who hath

---

[30] (Barfield, 1957, p. 179)

[31] (Barfield, 1977, p. 218)

ears. Barfield goes on to extend his picture of the consequences of such a "transition": [32]

> *Let us nevertheless suppose that the resistances are eventually overcome and try to imagine a second stage of transition. This surely must be a climate of extreme depression amounting in many quarters to despair . . . I am simply forced to envisage an epidemic of something like nervous breakdowns, with probably some suicides, within such solid fortresses of conformity as MIT or the London School of Economics and amongst their alumni.*

Interestingly, i.e., for the purposes of this book, in the same essay, "The Coming Trauma of Materialism", Barfield appeals to literature as the medium of choice to express any coming changes: [33]

> *One way or another there is an opportunity here for a good writer in the genre of science fiction by a really imaginative writer, who should fill out in terms of concrete events and experiences the issues I have merely glance at . . . If a society is really faced with startling changes and fairly imminent ones (and there is a good deal of evidence that ours is) it cannot be amiss for a few people here and there to be peering ahead, however inadequately, by way of preparation for them.*

While we may detect the echoes of tarning in the many rich metaphors of our language, the original act of tarning is an arduous and painstaking effort of an individual caught up in a process of *meaning* emerging into consciousness. The individual is thus, at first, mostly unconscious during this process of manifesting a possible future. Tarning happens to him or her as much as he or she makes it so. It is "an interpenetration . . . of spontaneous impulse and voluntary purpose . . . the potential works in them, even as the actual works on them!" [34]

---

[32]   Ibid: p. 228

[33]   Ibid: p. 229

[34]   Coleridge as quoted in (Barfield, 1967, p. 82)

From this deeper understanding of tarning, we are in a position to evaluate the modern examples I gave earlier.

To what degree and in what way are they really examples of tarning?

Clearly in all four examples, the human author had a voluntary purpose: Mandelbrot had discovered a new geometry and wanted to name it; Bernays brought together Freud's concept of unconscious desire and the political idea of controlling public opinion, in order to invent a discipline; Baljeu was keen to develop a theory of the physical, energetic, and spiritual make-up of the human being; Jung wanted to "rescue Meaning", i.e., the lost spiritual treasures of the past, by positing an unconscious "within" us that is the new locus of such treasures.

We may think of these conscious efforts as "projects"—the task that the author intends to carry out in the course of their efforts. [35]

Tarning, or the manifestation of a possible future, should not be seen simply as the *project* of the author, because, as well as voluntary purpose, tarning involves "spontaneous impulse", i.e., a possible future is *emerging* into consciousness and the author is usually quite unconscious of this aspect.

Subsequent beneficiaries of these authors' efforts most often simply agree to see things the same way the author does, i.e., only in terms of the conscious project or voluntary effort, and then to see the world in that way, as I said previously (Conditions 3 and 4).

Barfield addresses this crucial difference between conscious project and underlying, suggested meaning in his concept of *unresolved positivism*. He notes that our current modern reality is that of positivism (Cartesianism) in which an unbridgeable gap is felt between mental experience and the objective world "out there". Many writers today are attempting to overcome this gap by turning our attention to the putative interconnectedness of nature, or the inherent divinity of life, or the consciousness of nature etc.

---

[35]   With thanks to Wolfgang Giegerich—no tarning intended.

The belief seems to be that, by thinking these already conscious thoughts, we *in fact* overcome the positivism that is our modern reality: [36]

> *Unresolved positivism occurs when that conviction, that imagination, that way of looking at mind or body remains in fact in a man's mind even though he may have in philosophical theory rejected or resolved it.*

A simple example may illustrate this. Much research has gone into the evolution of consciousness and here seems to be general agreement that ancient consciousness was fundamentally different from our own, modern consciousness. We sense that our forbears were "intertwined" with or participated with their world in a way that is lost to us. They must have therefore lived in a fundamentally different world, too. Yet, our dominant theory of evolution rests on the premise that the world has been the same world for all time (Uniformitarianism) *and* that same world we are talking about is that world corresponding to *our* modern consciousness. In other words, while we may *talk* of participatory consciousness and the real world that correspond to that form of consciousness, we simultaneously unthinkingly support and subscribe to a world that is completely independent of any consciousness. [37] As Barfield remarks ironically: [38]

> . . . *out of all the wide variety of collective representations* [a term coined by Barfield to convey the inevitable polarity between consciousness and world] *which are found even today over the face of the earth, and the still wider variety which history unrolls before us, God has chosen for His delight the particular set shared by Western man in the last few centuries.*

---

[36] (Sugerman, 1976, p. 13)

[37] Uniformitarianism is the unprovable hypothesis proposed by Sir Charles Lyell that the laws of physics have been the same for all time. It is the basis of carbon dating, for example (the relative amount of carbon isotope being constant throughout time). Today we recognize that the world and our consciousness are somehow dependent on each other while simultaneously holding the view that the world is totally independent of our perceptions.

[38] (Barfield, 1957, p. 38)

Barfield's crucial distinction between voluntary effort and spontaneous impulse, along with his concept of unresolved positivism, approaches Wolfgang Giegerich's concept of the psychological difference. This concept points to the psychological fact that, while we may assert or claim certain viewpoints or worldviews (projects), our actual conduct in life is determined by the logical structure underpinning our consciousness. This underlying logical structure belongs to the time in which we are embedded, historically and we cannot change it, although we can relatively freely change our conscious worldviews. [39]

We can only "perceive" the possible future or emergent meaning that is emerging *through* these conscious projects by turning a *psychological* eye *to* the content but not fixed *on* the content, so that the content becomes transparent to the suggested new meaning that is seeking manifestation into actuality.

In Mandelbrot's case of tarning, we can easily see the voluntary purpose in his seeking a word to name his geometry. We can also "see" the spontaneous impulse in his less conscious move of casually leafing through the Latin dictionary that his son left on the table. In so doing, Mandelbrot discovered the word "fractus", which springs from an etymological root meaning "to break". From the cognates, "fraction" and "fragment" he coined the new word, fractal. We are now in the position of asking what possible future reality may be "seen" emerging, as suggested by the actions taken by Mandelbrot in this act of tarning.

Mandelbrot *coined* the word "fractal" from words which belong to a group that carry meanings of breaking, broken-ness, rubble, breaching, crushing, etc. This suggests to me that this is a similar process to other attempts made today to heal what is felt to be broken, or unbridgeable, by using a contrivance. For example, we hear of words such as "psychosomatic", the "mind-body" problem, "psychophysical", "mind-brain", and so on. We can get a clearer picture of this attempt to overcome the unbridgeable

---

[39] Giegerich's concept of the psychological difference is critical to understanding the complex nature of our modern consciousness. For a fuller discussion, see (Giegerich, 2001, p. 126), (Giegerich, Miller, & Mogenson, 2005, p. 111), (Giegerich, 2007b)

when we take a closer look at what was in the back of Mandelbrot's mind as he was working towards a name for his geometry.

In working towards his geometry of the irregular, such as a coastline, Mandelbrot realized that the length depended on "how close we are", or to put it another way, on the accuracy of the measuring instrument. The usual quantitative measurements (length, depth, thickness, etc.) failed to capture the essence of irregular shapes, since they all are relative to our distance from the object. Mandelbrot turned to the concept of dimension which uses whole numbers to define space—three representing our normal space of solid bodies, for example. So, if we take a ball of string, its dimension changes as we get closer (far away—0-D, closer—3-D, closer still—1-D, etc.) Mandelbrot was concerned with how the dimension of the object could change like that, abruptly between the whole numbers. To solve this geometrical problem Mandelbrot turned to fractions, which gave a "smooth transition". He could calculate the fractional dimensionality of his geometrical figures and that number proved constant over scale for a particular fractal representation of an irregular shape, like a coastline, or clouds—regular-irregularity. [40]

For our purposes we can see that the spontaneous impulse that was working in the background of his voluntary purpose concerned the overcoming of an unbridgeable difference (spatial dimension), just as neuroscience tries to overcome the gap between mind and body by coining "mind-brain", or as psychology attempts to overcome the split between self and world by inventing terms such as psychoid, or psychophysical, etc. The unbridgeable difference and its "overcoming" concerns our modern *reality* (called positivism, Cartesianism, etc.) and *possible futures* that are emerging, constituting new forms of consciousness that "overcome" positivism.

We can see the same background spontaneous impulse in Bernays' example of tarning. His voluntary purpose, as we have seen, was to establish a discipline (Public Relations) which manipulates the unconscious desire of ordinary people for the sake of shaping public opinion (propaganda). Here we can see the same logic of difference working in the background of Bernays' thought, without which it would have been impossible to

---

[40]   (Gleick, 1997, p. 97 ff)

conceive Public Relations. Desire, for example once belonged to the gods who subjected us to their will in order to fulfil their desires. I think of poor Paris in this regard. He was forced to choose the most beautiful among the three goddesses, who simply desired he do so. It was in the nature of a game for them. However, this game had deadly consequences for human beings, with the ten year-long Trojan War that followed. Desire since descended into human beings with the inevitable consequence of a new definition of man (*my* desires, *my* thoughts, *my* will etc.) but an invisible connection (interpenetration) with the spiritual realm still being part of that definition (the Great Chain of Being) until the 19th century when it was finally severed. [41]

With Bernays, we are able to see that desire is now a commodity, a thing that can be manipulated. The particular nature or quality of desire (fear, longing, erotic, etc.) is only important in so far as it influences the form of manipulation—e.g. what particular images are needed in the advertising etc. Desire no longer has any intrinsic worth, nor has any connection with a divine background to life. Similarly, people have been reduced to items side by side on a production line, whose only discernible quality lies in their numerical difference. This is a totally new definition of man that is working in the background of Bernays thought, as well as all those that followed. We can get a feel for this background by noting that when Bernays discovered that Goebbels was using his theory for his own purposes in Nazi Germany, he was shocked. [42] The only reason he *could* be shocked is that his voluntary purpose was dissociated in his mind from the spontaneous impulse working within the tarning.

Jung's efforts in writing *The Red Book* also involved his voluntary purpose (the content of *The Red Book*) and the spontaneous impulse working through the content as its only possible medium of expression (tarning). Only by carefully exploring the exact nature of Jung's participation in the creation of *The Red Book* can we begin to discern a possible future manifesting through the efforts of Jung, unbeknownst to him or anyone else in the Jungian community, with one exception, as I noted above (see footnote 25).

---

[41]   (Tillyard, 1942)

[42]   (Bernays, 1965)

It is striking to me that only one subsequent analyst has turned his and our attention to the content of *The Red Book* as a magnificent example of tarning (or of the psychological difference, to use Giegerich's formulation), where the content is understood as a *medium of expression* of the otherwise invisible spontaneous impulse (new meaning, possible future). Wolfgang Giegerich has shown that the text of *The Red Book* reveals a decades-long painful process in which Jung was drawn into installing, or fabricating (the underlying logical structure of) a new reality (possible future) that has little to do with his voluntary purpose of establishing the concept of the familiar Jungian unconscious.

This possible future has not been noticed by future commentators, until Wolfgang Giegerich, probably because of a lack of awareness of the process of tarning by which new meaning or new forms of reality come into existence. But this reality has been imitated, and the four conditions necessary for the manifestation of a shared and real future have been met. This possible future, far from being continuous with the shared Jungian worldview developed from *The Red Book* by Jung and then others, is completely dissociated, yet remains determinative of real actions in the world, as we shall now see.

Jung's conscious conception of the unconscious is as I said based exclusively on his voluntary purpose (project) of *The Red Book*, with no attention given to its unconscious spontaneous impulse (underlying logic) that structures the content of *The Red Book* in the first place. It is only by giving attention to this underlying logic lying within the content of *The Red Book* that we are able to apperceive the possible future that *actually* comes into being through Jung's participation in making *The Red Book*.

Giegerich takes up this approach in his review of Shamdasani's book, *Jung and the Making of Modern Psychology*. [43] He asks: [44]

> *The question emerges for us how and why the unconscious did come to be conceived as a natural object (thereby opening up the project of rescuing god, or Meaning). The precondition was the*

---

[43]   (Shamdasani, 2003)

[44]   (Giegerich, 2004, p. 209)

> *great revolution from the metaphysical* [i.e. what Barfield calls
> the Aristotelan mindscape] *to the positivisitc, scientistic stance
> at the beginning of the 19ᵗʰ century . . . the unconscious is the
> return . . . of the memory of and longing for metaphysics under
> the conditions of positivity.*

Giegerich's review of *The Red Book* appeared soon after in Spring Journal.
[45] This review is the first and only one that examines the logical structure
that underlies and *forms* the content that comprises *The Red Book*, when
viewed psychologically. A certain preparation however, is needed in order
to know how to approach this article and indeed *The Red Book* in order to
grasp Giegerich's arguments and, finally, his conclusion.

When we dream and then wake up, the usual response on the part of
the waking or empirical ego is to identify with the stance of the dream
ego, and then to base one's understanding of the dream on that particular
stance. Furthermore, many people base subsequent action in the world
on the dream ego's stance in the dream. However, It would be a fatal
methodological mistake of the part of any psychologist of the soul to also
take up the stance of the dream ego as the only one to consider when
working with the dream: [46]

> *Psychologically it is a grave mistake to privilege one element
> of a dream, fantasy, or psychic experience, for example the I,
> taking it literally by setting it up as a given existing outside the
> fantasy . . .*

In other words, when we approach a dream or indeed *The Red Book* as a
soul phenomenon, we must regard equally every aspect of the fantasies in
order to understand them psychologically.

The results of doing just that are startling indeed and Giegerich's long
article is very persuasive in that it shows that "empirical" Jung i.e. Jung the
dreamer identified solely with the *I* that appears within the fantasies, when
he drew his conclusions about the nature of the unconscious. But if *we*

---

[45]   (Giegerich, 2010)

[46]   Ibid: p. 372.

pay equal attention to what Jung himself says *as the internal other*, i.e., as the *other* also appearing within the fantasy, a completely different picture emerges. I'll focus on just one aspect that demonstrates the nature of the possible future that pressed forward as a spontaneous impulse through Jung's voluntary effort (i.e. the content of *The Red Book*).

As Giegerich shows, Jung repeatedly, from *within* the fantasies, meets the figures appearing to him with a denial of their reality: *within* the fantasy where the *I* is merely one figure among others in the same fiction, Jung says, "surely you are symbols", "I am convinced that *Izdubar* is not at all real in the ordinary sense but a fantasy . . ." As Giegerich says: [47]

> *Jung enters his fantasies with the categories of external reflection, namely with the distinction between fantasy and reality. Inside his fantasies, he views them from the outside and doubts the reality of their figures. It is as if a novel tried to pull the rug out from under its characters as only imagined, or as if we, while dreaming, turned around to the wild animal or to the murderous criminal chasing us and said to them, 'you are only symbols'.*

This means that Jung developed the capacity to enter his fantasies as the empirical I, able to view, from within his fantasies, *other figures as positive objects*! In this way he was able to simulate outer positive reality, *from within the fantasies*.

Jung unconsciously participated in fabricating a domain of reality that *simulates* outer modern reality (positivism, Cartesianism). The Jungian unconscious is *not* in reality a recapitulation of former ages in which reality has imaginal depth, but is a simulation of positivity, our modern structure of consciousness, the background logic of our existence over which we have no control. It is determinative!

Giegerich shows how Jung internalized the images of the natural or mental cosmos that formerly surrounded us, but did so under modern conditions of positivity, thereby constructing an "inner" that simulates

---

[47]   Ibid: p. 402.

modern empirical reality. It was a long, extraordinarily painful process, to the point of torture and madness, involving a kind of turning inside out of reality, or rather a turning outside in. [48]

In so doing, Jung, through the process of turning, brought into being a reality that is a fabricated *simulation* of the outer empirical world of positivism. He unwittingly became a mouthpiece of this possible future and it has continued to manifest through the efforts of others, as well, independently of Jung.

At this time millions of people are *logging on* in order to participate in virtual or simulated reality (*Second Life, Sim City, interactive games* etc.), a product of our technological civilization. They enter a realm of image and interact with other images, *as* an image (avatar). Now we do this also on a daily basis when we dream or when we read a book. You could say that the empirical *I* becomes the fictional *I*, much like Alice is portrayed in Wonderland. So what is different with these technological worlds of simulation? When Alice drops into Wonderland, she leaves the categories of thought that belong to empirical reality behind and becomes fictional herself, evaluating this new reality within its own terms (remember her long conversations with the caterpillar and Humpty Dumpty for example). In fact when she does at the end employ an *empirical* category of thought, "O, you all are just a pack of cards!" she moves out of fictional reality back into empirical reality where she becomes a little girl once more. While she was inside the fiction, as a fictional figure, each character opens up to its own interiority and depth, its own truth.

In contrast, when we enter *Second Life* this does not happen. Instead, we enter as the *empirical I*, carrying with us all our empirical categories of thought. We know and do not forget that the avatar we meet on the street is a construction, like our own avatar, an "object", like empirical objects, only in the form of an image *positivized*. These images have no inner depth, or interiority. Any imaginal nature has been destroyed altogether. In other words we do not relate to a user's avatar in the way Alice relates to the imaginal figures of Wonderland. No one asks a Celtic warrior avatar about his initiation; his battles, his losses, his wisdom etc. Images are treated as

---

[48]   (Giegerich, 2010)

empirical objects, related to by the empirical ego, *from within the fantasy*, with its empirical categories of thought.

This is exactly analogous to lucid dreaming in which the fictional ego "wakes up" within the dream into its status as empirical ego and applies its categories of thought to what it then sees: "O, these are all just symbols or dream images. I can do anything I want. I'll try flying etc."

This is the psychology of simulated or fabricated reality! Fabricated reality *is* a reality—one that simulates positive reality *in the realm of images itself* (the imagination). Images are regarded with categories of thought that properly belong to empirical reality, and regarded as such from within imaginal reality itself.

When we make the distinction between the content (voluntary purpose) of *The Red Book* and the way its content is structured (the spontaneous impulse that informs the content), we can thus see that two dissociated conceptions of reality emerge in the Jungian project. The content speaks of the unconscious as the new, private domain of reality, which recapitulates the phenomenology of the public reality of former ages (immediacy, objectivity, autonomy, truth, epiphany, divinity, meaning, etc.) This conception is accepted by subsequent generations of people who agreed to see things the same way, leading to the establishment of cultural forms (Jungian Analysis and so on) that teach others to see things the same way: the Jungian unconscious. This reality may more properly be called a conscious *worldview* that can compete with other worldviews in the public market of meanings today.

A careful psychological analysis of the spontaneous impulse of *The Red Book* leads to a very different conception of reality, a *fabricated* reality, one that simulates our outer positivistic reality, within the world of image. Unbeknownst to Jung and the generations that followed, Jung participated in the formation of the logical structure that underlies what later came to be known as *simulated reality*, a reality that truly belongs to our modern technological age, giving rise, for example, to the possibility of television. [49] This reality *is* a reality, i.e., determinative of our modern existence, not

---

[49] (Giegerich, 2007b)

merely a worldview, and as such may properly be called a possible future manifesting into actuality through the efforts of the man Jung. In this way we may see that *The Red Book* truly shows a process of tarning taking place.

It is particularly illuminating to turn to the mass media today to find a "text" that completely confirms, demonstrates, and even applauds the logic of simulated reality, that same possible future that Jung brought into existence through his "confrontation with the unconscious" as recorded in *The Red Book*.

The 2009 smash hit movie *Avatar* points to a lost world of our past, a nostalgic longing for a natural world saturated with spiritual meaning. The native inhabitants live in perfect harmony with nature. This world is colonized by exploitative humans who proceed to mine the planet for its mineral riches, destroying the lives of the innocent natives, as well as their habitat. The content of the movie appealed greatly to our current longing for former times in our own history when we supposedly had a much more intimate connection with nature which was felt to be alive, and conscious. The plot even proposes that a return to such a pristine existence is possible through the use of technology, in particular, avatars!

Today tens of millions of people are now online, *doing* what the movie represents so well with an astonishing acceptance of its ordinariness. The fact that millions on a daily basis are doing what the movie proposes as a possibility may account for the easy acceptance of the movie's premise and central symbol (*Avatar*!). Millions, maybe tens of millions now, are entering their own avatar in order to inhabit another world for as long as they like.

However, if we turn a psychological eye to the "text" of the movie, i.e., to the logical structure underlying and permeating the content of the movie, another picture looms up behind.

This is not a movie about a lost innocence. It is training manual for the West, urging us to go further in what we can already do: enter an avatar and go into, not nature, but cyberspace. *Avatar* is the common name known to millions of "gamers" who daily enter "Planet Pandora" and engage in the same impossible feats that are shown in the movie. The beautiful images have no correspondence at all with nature on earth, past or present, and are merely the scientific means (graphics, 3-D etc.) by which the modern ego is captivated and seduced into leaving earthly reality and entering cyberspace, perhaps forever, as our hero did. But we should note well: when he did succeed in becoming a Pandorian resident, his earthly body *died*!

This is no mere fantasy. Millions are doing it already. This movie simply acts as an openly seductive *engine*, in the best spirit of Public Relations, designed to encourage a particular "solution" to our loss of meaning and isolation. Our collective nostalgia for the past, a *fancied* innocence, and primordial oneness etc. is simply the "unconscious desire" that can be caught and manipulated towards other ends, as the public relations industry knows so well. For all those who think it is about nature and rediscovering our interconnectedness, I would urge them to remember how our hero enters Pandora: he lies in a coffin and "dies" just as millions do when they log on. They die to the ordinary world and their bodies waste away as they spend twelve or sixteen hours online in cyberspace enjoying their freedom—freedom from ordinary reality which is becoming harder to bear as we witness the accelerating emptying out of meaning in the natural world!

Avatar is a movie spelling out the method and encouraging what millions really want to do—escape earthly reality altogether and enter cyberspace, at the cost of earthly life altogether. As determined by its logical structure or syntax, *Avatar* is decidedly *not* a movie showing us how to reclaim our interconnectedness and oneness with nature. Pandora is not a representation of nature at all. It is a true and accurate representation of what we are already building and investing billions of dollars in: cyberspace or virtual reality which *is* a reality indeed but *not* a natural one—it is a fabricated one! The entire engine of our modern technological society is now geared towards the invention of cyberspace into which we are now *openly* being invited. We are to inhabit it in exactly the way shown by the movie, leaving behind, as the movie also shows us, a dead earth and a dead body.

This movie is only one example of cultural forms emerging in our times that accurately reflect and strengthen the dissociation between the consciously held conception (Jung's "recovery of lost innocence") and the underlying logical structure of a possible future that is fast becoming a shared and real existence (fabricated or simulated reality).

The Red Book thus provides us with a soul phenomenon ("dream" text) that beautifully exemplifies the four conditions I outlined above involved in the process of tarning. We can also describe the process as one in which the human mind participates in the self-transformation of the living logic that determines the next forms of reality. We are still in a great state of flux as I said earlier—many forms of reality seem to be "incarnating" at this time. I want to repeat the four conditions here:

1. The individual effort of participation with an aspect of possible futures;
2. The individual as mouthpiece of this future;
3. The willingness on the part of others to make a move towards seeing the world the same way the individual does;
4. The gradual congealing of that "way of seeing" into that way the world is seen, the world becoming "that way".

We can see that Jung's ordeal as recorded in *The Red Book* was such a participation in the logical life of the soul as it restructured itself as the logic of fabricated reality (Condition 1). He then propagated this new form of reality through teachings and writing albeit quite unconsciously (Condition 2). Jung believed he was promoting a quite different conception of the unconscious, as we have seen (his voluntary purpose or project). Others took up his conception and likewise propagated it further, also paying no attention to the underlying spontaneous impulse that was working its way further into manifestation *through* the conscious content. They thus also participated in the logic that gives rise to fabricated reality (Condition 3). Cultural forms that enact and reinforce that logic in actual deeds then sprung up and we are approaching that time when we are moving from this "way of seeing" to "that way the world is seen" (Condition 4).

TARNING AND LITERATURE

We are living in a time when many possible futures are seeking manifestation through our more or less conscious participation in the process that Barfield names as tarning. The first forms that appear when reality is transforming, are artistic ones and today Contemporary Art demonstrates the multiplicity of possibilities: [50]

> [C]ontemporary art is no longer one kind of art, nor does it have a limited set of shared qualities somewhat distinct from those of the art of past periods in the history of art yet fundamentally continuous with them.
>
> It does not presume inevitable historical development; it has no expectation that present confusion will eventually cohere into a style representative of this historical moment. Such art is multiple, internally differentiating, category-shifting, shape-changing, unpredictable (that is, diverse)—like contemporaneity itself.

We have seen that C. G. Jung's *Liber Novus* (*The Red Book*) is a form of literature that Jung understood as *"writing autobiographical material but not as an autobiography."* We have further seen that Wolfgang Giegerich's analysis shows *The Red Book* to be a form of literature that involves *tarning* throughout, unbeknownst to Jung and, it seems, most other auditors of the book subsequent to its publication. There is no genre of literature available at present to categorise such a book. As Giegerich demonstrates, *The Red Book*, as a record of tarning, shows how a possible future (in this

---

[50]   (Smith, 2011, p. 9)

case fabricated or simulated reality) may manifest *through* the voluntary purpose of the author who may be quite unconscious of that process. Giegerich notes that, as recorded in *The Red Book*, Jung's experience of this manifestation of the spontaneous impulse: [51]

> . . . *is a process which to a large extent has the nature of painful suffering and torment (up the point of near-madness) and is accordingly experienced as "cruel", a very frequent word in The Red Book.*

Jung also describes his experience of this process of manifestation: [52]

> *I was so frequently wrought up that I had to do certain yoga exercises in order to hold my emotions in check. But since it was my purpose to know what was going on within myself, I would do these exercises only until I has calmed myself enough to resume my work with the unconscious. As soon as I had the feeling that I was myself again, I abandoned this restraint upon the emotions and allowed the images and inner voices to speak afresh . . . .*
>
> *To the extent that I managed to translate the emotions into images—that is to say, to find the images which were concealed in the emotions—I was inwardly calmed and reassured. Had I left those images hidden in the emotions, I might have been torn to pieces by them.*

He reports that on one occasion: [53]

> . . . *I tried to follow the same procedure, but it would not descend. I remained on the surface. Then I realized I had a conflict within myself about going down, but I could not make out what it was* (the conflict then appeared to Jung as an image of two serpents fighting, one retired defeated and the

---

[51]   (Giegerich, 2010, pp. 391-392)

[52]   (Jung, 1963, p. 177)

[53]   (Jung, 1989, pp. 96-97)

fantasy then deepened) . . . I saw the snake approach me . . . the coils reached up to my heart. I realized as I struggled, that I had assumed the attitude of the Crucifixion. In the agony and the struggle, I sweated so profusely that the water flowed down on all sides of me . . . I felt my face had taken on the face of an animal of prey, a lion or a tiger.

Jung later comments: [54]

You cannot get conscious of these unconscious facts without giving yourself to them. If you can overcome your fear of the unconscious and let yourself down, then these facts take on a life of their own. You can be gripped by these ideas so that you really go mad, or nearly so. These images have so much reality that they recommend themselves, and so much extraordinary meaning that one is caught.

These reports come subsequent to the writing of *The Red Book* and as such are memories of Jung's experience. The following passage, however, occurs within *The Red Book*. Jung is confronted within a vision, by a murdered child and a woman standing by, whose face is covered by a veil. To his horror, the woman demands that he eat the liver of the child. He does so:[55]

I kneel down on the stone, cut off a piece of the liver and put it in my mouth. My gorge rises—tears burst from my eyes—cold sweat covers my brow—a dull sweet taste of blood—I swallow with desperate efforts—it is impossible—once again and once again—I almost faint—it is done. The horror has been accomplished.

We are not here merely reading an imaginative account of what it would be like to eat the liver of a murdered little girl. As such we could compare this graphic description with many other, equally compelling, and perhaps

---

54   Ibid

55   (Jung, 2009, p. 290)

even fascinating horror stories such as those by Edgar Allen Poe, or even Dante's journey through *Inferno*.

We are instead witnessing a first-hand account of the actual experience of the *empirical* Jung while *in the realm of fantasy*. Jung is not in the fantasy as a fictional *I* as Dante was in *The Divine Comedy*, but as the empirical *I*. *The Red Book* is analogous to reading a diary of a grotesque first-hand report of an actual act of cannibalism with the unheard-of twist that here, while Jung's reactions are empirical, the act is fictional!

There is a well-known widely defined form of literature called Magical Realism in which the process which Jung went through in actuality is explored *fictionally*. Magical Realism explores the impact fictional reality has on ordinary reality or, as C. S. Lewis puts it in reference to the books of Charles Williams, the effect of the "marvelous" invading the ordinary:[56]

> [In Williams' novels]: *We meet, on the one hand, very ordinary modern people who talk the slang of our own day and who live in the suburbs. On the other hand we also meet the supernatural—ghosts, magicians, and archetypal beasts. The first thing to grasp is that this not a mixture of two literary kinds. That's what some readers suspect and resent. They acknowledge on the one hand straight fiction: the classical novel, as we know it from Fielding to Goldsworthy. They acknowledge on the other the pure fantasy which creates a world of its own cut off in a kind of ringed fence, from reality—books like Wind in the Willows . . . and they complain that Williams is asking them to skip to and fro from one to the other in the same work. But Williams is really writing a third kind of book which belongs to neither class and has a different value from either. He is writing that sort of book in which we begin by saying, "Let us suppose that this everyday world were at some one point invaded by the marvelous".*

---

[56]   (Lewis, 2012)

Williams' books brilliantly describe the process of manifestation as purely fictional realities "invade" empirical reality: [57]

> *She was where he had left her, but a dreadful change was coming over her. Her body was writhing into curves and knots where she lay, as if cramps convulsed her. Her mouth was open, but she could not scream; her hands were clutching at her twisted throat. In her wide eyes there was now no malice, only an agony, and gradually all her body and head were drawn up backwards from the floor by an invisible force, so that from the hips she remained rigidly upright and her legs lay stretched straight out behind her upon the ground, as if a serpent in human shape raised itself before him . . .*

> *The face rounded out till it was perfectly smooth, with no hollows or depressions, and from her nostrils and her mouth something was thrusting out. In and out of her neck and hands an—other skin was forming, over or under her own—he could not distinguish which, but growing through it, here a coating, there an underveiling. Another and an inhuman tongue was flicking out over a human face . . .*

This is a graphic and vivid description quite analogous to the manifestation that Jung endured with *Leontocephalus*, which I will repeat here:

> *. . . I saw the snake approach me . . . the coils reached up to my heart. I realized as I struggled, that I had assumed the attitude of the Crucifixion. In the agony and the struggle, I sweated so profusely that the water flowed down on all sides of me . . . I felt my face had taken on the face of an animal of prey, a lion or a tiger.*

Both Williams and Jung are describing a process in which a purely fictional figure manifests in the empirical human being, the crucial difference being that William's "empirical human being" is also fictional (a character in a

---

[57]   (Williams, 2003, p. 170)

story) whereas, for Jung it was happening to him, in empirical reality, *from within the fiction.*

The difference in the genres could also be expressed this way. The *character* in Williams' novel is going through the cruel transformation but it is unlikely that Williams the author went through it as well. Jung, however, *did* go through his own version of the experience that Williams' character went through, while he was recording the experience or shortly after: [58]

> *I had no choice but to write everything down in the style selected by the unconscious itself. Sometimes it was as if I were hearing it with my ears, sometimes feeling it with my mouth, as if my tongue were formulating words; now and then I heard myself whispering aloud. Below the threshold of consciousness everything was seething with life.*

For Jung the fictional figures gained such a life that: [59]

> *At times he seemed to me quite real as if he* [i.e. Philemon—one of many purely fictional figures that came to Jung's attention] *were a living personality. I went walking up and down the garden with him, and to me he was what the Indians call a guru.*

We can even emphasise the difference further by noting that Williams and other authors of the broadly defined genre of Magical Realism would probably not have the concern that Jung had, as expressed by him: [60]

> *The more the images are realized, the more you will be gripped by them. When the images come to you and are not understood, you are in the society of the gods or, if you will, the lunatic society; you are no longer in human society, for you cannot express yourself. Only when you can say, "This image is so and so," only then do you remain in human society. Anybody could*

---

[58] (Jung, 1963, p. 178)

[59] Ibid, p. 183

[60] (Jung, 1989, p. 99)

> *be caught by these things and lost in them—some throw the*
> *experience away saying it is all nonsense, and thereby losing*
> *their best value, for these are the creative images. Another may*
> *identify himself with the images and become a crank or a fool.*

Whereas C. S. Lewis referred to a genre of writing (Magical Realism) in which the marvellous invades the ordinary within the *fictional*, Jung's *Liber Novus* (*The Red Book*) is a record of this fictional invasion happening to him, the author, *empirically*: [61]

> *Around five o'clock in the afternoon on Sunday the front door*
> *bell began ringing frantically . . . there was no one in sight . . .*
> *The whole house was filled as if there were a crowd present,*
> *crammed full of spirits . . . then it all began to flow out of me*
> *and in the course of three evenings the thing was written* [Septem
> Sermones—The Seven Sermons of the Dead]. *As soon as I*
> *took up the pen, the whole ghostly assemblage evaporated. The*
> *room quieted and the atmosphere cleared. The haunting was*
> *over . . . It was an unconscious constellation* [i.e. invasion] *. . .*
> *the numen of an archetype* [the marvellous)] *. . . The intellect,*
> *of course, would . . . like to write the whole thing off as a*
> *violation of the rules. But what a dreary world* [the ordinary]
> *it would be if the rules were not violated sometimes!*

The new, as yet unnamed genre of literature that Jung seems to have inaugurated, involves *"writing autobiographical material but not as an autobiography."* It also is a process of tarning in which a new form of reality (possible future) manifests through the (mostly unconscious) efforts of the individual. If the four conditions I outlined above are fulfilled then that possible future may become our reality. We saw that this process of tarning was at work to some degree in the other examples I cited as well as in Jung's *Liber Novus*.

The possible future that began to manifest through Jung's efforts, as recorded in *The Red Book*, is that of fabricated or simulated reality—that

---

[61]   (Jung, 1963, pp. 190-191)

form of reality that subsequently has been reinforced in the realm of technology: [62]

> *The purpose of* [relating to purely fictional figure in terms of categories that belong to empirical reality] *is to set it* [i.e. fiction] *as absolutely real in a naturalistic or positivistic (already reflected) sense. Fantasy has to* simulate *the character of hard-core reality for its fictions . . . much like the new 20*[th] *century* technical *medium of movies simulates reality so convincingly as to fool everyone.*

---

[62] (Giegerich, 2010, p. 403)

TARNING AND
EMPIRICAL REALITY

There are many ways that our modern structure of consciousness can be characterized today. They all have in common the description of a split, dissociation, abyss, disjunction, gap, between different components of that structure, within the structure. Speaking in terms of an empirical-fictional dichotomy is therefore simply one other way to describe our modern consciousness. We all know the difference between fact and fiction in literature, for example, or non-fiction and fiction. Magical Realism is a genre of literature which portrays the fictional intruding into empirical life, as in the work of Charles Williams. Another compelling example is that of Stephen Marlowe who tells the story of the missing seven days of Edgar Allen Poe's life (i.e. no documented accounts of his whereabouts seem to be available) shortly before he died. [63] Marlowe's novel "melds fact and fantasy to transform fiction in a work of towering talent and illumination". [64]

Within this fictional account, Marlowe crafts a scene in which Poe is talking with the character of Dupin, a detective of Poe's own creation. It is not unusual of course for an author to engage their own figures of the imagination the same way we engage persons in empirical life. The disturbing element occurs when fictional Dupin begins to engage with people (a Dr. Moran and his wife) who are on the same side of reality as Poe, i.e., the empirical side (as such within this story). He sees them come

---

[63]   (Marlowe, 1996)

[64]   Ibid: Back Cover

into Poe's room and he and Poe talk afterwards about them. Later on, Dr. Moran is hurrying along a passageway when he hears footsteps pounding towards him. He sees no one. Something crashes him against a wall where he falls down. He sees an object on the ground and picks it up. He has a pair of spectacles, twisted and shattered. They belong, unbeknownst to Moran, to Dupin. [65]

From the examples of Williams and Marlowe, we can see that such ingenious provocative and disturbing writing that goes by the name of Magical Realism, is only possible for a consciousness that is structured in a way that empirical reality is separated from fictional reality by a gulf.

This structure is a historical phenomenon and in order to understand this more fully, as well as to begin to comprehend the exact nature of tarning today, as the manifestation of possible futures, we need to approach that historical time when empirical reality and fictional reality (modern terms with meanings that correspond only to our modern structure of consciousness) were not so separated.

It is well known that the scientific revolution inaugurated a new structure of consciousness and world in which the imagination was separated out from empirical reality according to the distinction between quality and quantity. Qualities of objects began to be understood as belonging to the subject while quantity belonged to the outer object.

We can turn to literature to get a feel for the way things were prior to that separation. Literature can take us back into former structures of consciousness that we have superseded today. When I read Nicolai Tolstoy's *The Coming of the King*, I am taken *into* that time in which *what we would call* empirical and fictional realities were co-extensive to a degree that is impossible for us today. For the Celts at that time, it was simply *reality*. [66]

---

[65] Ibid: p. 323

[66] (Tolstoy, 1989)

Merlin and his companion Rufinus, a Roman tribune, are climbing a hill, engaging in animated conversation. As they climb, wild nature begins to encroach and civilised life fades in the distance. [67]

> *The air was raw and chilly, and cold had arisen upon a wind blowing the full length of the world from the hard unyielding planets set in the void above Dinleu Gurygon. The rough shoulder of the hill against which I leaned felt icy cold, and icy cold was I becoming myself . . . Rufinus was speaking, but I could feel the draw and power of the hill exerted upon me, and his words became faint and distant. Other sounds were replacing those of his broken Ladin speech. A nightjar, twisting silently in the night sky above us, uttered a guttural "churr, churr" from his great gaping mouth; like the tribune, he was newly come from Africa, and like the tribune his voice was harsh and broken. From all about me in the heather and upon the rocks came a rustling and squeaking and grunting . . . I heard bats squeaking in the rimy dark and felt faint breeze upon my face from the wings of blundering moths. The cold had become yet more bitter: cold, cold, cold. I felt as if I were frozen into the hard ground, like the exposed outcrop against which I leaned for support. The owl's discordant shriek heralded the rising of a night mist, a vapor from each hollow, an encircling gray hood about the hilltop. I did not doubt that it was the mist of Gwyn mab Nud, smoky unguent of the Witches of Annufn, a shaggy mantle over the land . . .*
>
> *I was wedged in the belly of the hill, my body stiff, cold, and inert. Before me, cross-legged upon a mound, sat a huge skin-clad herdsman, beside him a curly-haired mastiff bigger than a stallion of nine winters. Its breath was such that it would consume dead wood and yellowed tufts of grass upon the open Plain of Powys beneath. In his hand the great swart figure bore an iron club that would be a burden for two men to carry.*

---

[67]   Ibid: p. 254 ff.

Here we can see a seamless transition from ordinary reality to "the marvellous", as C. S. Lewis puts it. No intrusion, no invasion, no penetration. Ordinary reality simply recedes and what *we* might call fictional reality assumes ascendancy.

The spiritual tradition that Tolstoy's *Merlin* has mastered reaches back at least to the time of Parmenides. The central practice of initiates is that of the *Iatromantis*, or *Phôlarchos*, a practice of incubation that opened one up to spiritual reality. The practice simply involved crawling into a lair and "collapsing" or becoming still, while staying awake. Spiritual reality is simply there, waiting for us. Merlin entered this state and found the mythic Herdsman already there waiting for him. [68]

As we know, that mythic world has come to an end and we may look for literary works like Tolstoy's novel that can also take us into an experience of the world at the "moment" of its ending. Cervantes' *Don Quixote* is such a book. It tells a story of a man for whom the imaginal richness of the world is still alive, while all around him, others have left that world and now inhabit our modern empirical world. Here is a scene where Don Quixote ("The Knight of the Rueful Countenance") is on an adventure with his servant ("squire"): [69]

> *At this point they came in sight of thirty forty windmills that there are on plain, and as soon as Don Quixote saw them he said to his squire, "Fortune is arranging matters for us better than we could have shaped our desires ourselves, for look there, friend Sancho Panza, where thirty or more monstrous giants present themselves, all of whom I mean to engage in battle and slay, and with whose spoils we shall begin to make our fortunes; for this is righteous warfare, and it is God's good service to sweep so evil a breed from off the face of the earth."*

> *"What giants?" said Sancho Panza.*

---

[68] (Kingsley, 2001, p. 108 ff)

[69] (de Cervantes, 1997)

"Those thou seest there," answered his master, "with the long arms, and some have them nearly two leagues long."

"Look, your worship," said Sancho; "what we see there are not giants but windmills, and what seem to be their arms are the sails that turned by the wind make the millstone go."

"It is easy to see," replied Don Quixote, "that thou art not used to this business of adventures; those are giants; and if thou art afraid, away with thee out of this and betake thyself to prayer while I engage them in fierce and unequal combat."

The imaginal world and the world that came into being with the scientific revolution, bringing with it a division between empirical world (the real world) and the imaginal world (now downgraded to fiction) can thus be seen to be fundamentally different. This difference has been beautifully captured by Owen Barfield: [70]

If, with the help of some time-machine working in reverse, a man of the Middle Ages could be suddenly transported into the skin of a man of the twentieth century, seeing through our eyes and with our 'figuration' the objects we see, I think he would feel like a child who looks for the first time at a photograph through the ingenious magic of a stereoscope. 'Oh!' he would say, 'look how they stand out!' We must not forget that in his time perspective had not yet been discovered, nor underrate the significance of this . . . Before the scientific revolution the world was more like a garment men wore about them than a stage on which they moved. In such a world the convention of perspective was unnecessary. To such a world other conventions of visual reproduction, such as the nimbus and the halo, were as appropriate as to ours they are not. It was as if the observers were themselves in the picture. Compared with us, they felt themselves and the objects around them and the words that expressed those objects, immersed together in something like a clear lake of-what shall we say?—of 'meaning'.

---

[70]   (Barfield, 1957, p. 94)

Empirical reality is now privileged as *reality* and the former *imaginal* reality, as described above, and by Barfield, is now downgraded to fiction, a lesser reality, one that does not carry the same conviction of *reality* in the way that empirical reality does. [71]

With this clear demarcation in place, we are now in a position to return to the genre of Magical Realism, and Jung's *Liber Novus*, and the astonishing soul movement portrayed as fictional reality bursting into, or invading, empirical reality.

Wolfgang Giegerich brings our attention to a compelling and popular icon of the early 20th century:

This famous poster by James Montgomery Flagg: [72]

---

[71]   For a fuller discussion of the archetypal basis of the division between empirical reality and fictional reality, see (Giegerich, 2007b): *The Rocket and the Launching Base, or The Leap from the Imaginal into the Outer Space Named "Reality"*.

[72]   Ibid: p. 121

> *. . . shows a man dressed as Uncle Sam who points with his finger directly at the viewer saying, "I want YOU". Something extraordinary is happening here . . . The* [fictional] *person . . . breaks out of his containment within the fictional or imaginal world of the picture into the literal "external"* [empirical] *reality where the flesh-and-blood viewers live.*

Giegerich goes on to remind us that this instance of penetration by the fictional into empirical reality is itself fictional, i.e., not literally so: [73]

> *But the poster of Uncle Sam is and remains a poster, an image. The Uncle Sam represented there does not in fact step out of the picture to us, the audience. He only appears to do so as long as we for our part look at the poster naturally, imaginally: are seduced into its aura. The busting of the image occurs in the image and as image.*

There are modern forms of theatre and performance art in which a more literal penetration into empirical reality is taking place. The audience is no longer seduced by the art *into* the reality of the play but is often addressed directly by the characters that even interact physically with the audience. Jung's descriptions of his own experiences as recorded in *The Red Book* show a similar process in which purely fictional figures impress *their* reality (which has historically been downgraded to a status of "not real") on the empirical Jung with great convincing power.

While, as I said, the genre of Magical Realism shows the penetration of fictional reality into empirical reality *within* the fictional form (as the Uncle Sam poster does), it seems to me that modern performance or participatory art, as well as Jung's *Liber Novus*, are showing an further development in this movement.

I would suggest that works such as Charles Williams are of the order of an *intuition* of a soul movement that is a development from the centuries-long split between empirical reality and fictional reality. This historical split, also a determinative soul movement, has the consequence of privileging

---

[73]   Ibid: p. 133

"outer" reality, the reality of surfaces, i.e., empiricism, and, at the same time, downgrading "inner" reality to what we now call fiction, or the imagination, to a status of "unreal".

I further suggest that the soul is engaging in a movement to transform this relationship between empirical reality and fictional reality. This soul movement is a modern form of tarning in which a possible future is manifesting through the efforts of individuals—such as C. G. Jung.

The immense difficulty in comprehending this movement can be seen in Jung's efforts to comprehend what was happening to him. As I noted above, Wolfgang Giegerich's analysis of *The Red Book* shows that the possible future manifesting through C. G. Jung is a fabricated reality, a simulated *empirical* reality. I believe this conception, while certainly being a step along the way, as it were, needs refinement in order to fully comprehend this next soul movement that seems to be transforming the relationship between empirical reality and fictional reality. The intrusion of fictional reality into Jung's empirical life is simply an exemplary instance of what I believe to be a growing phenomenon throughout the world today.

THE NEW REALITY:
A Unity of Empirical Reality and Fictional Reality

There is a world-wide movement called *The International Community for Hearing Voices* now in its 13th year, while another called the *Hearing Voices Network* is in its 25th year (2012). [74] [75]

These movements grew out of an astonishing re-evaluation of the nature of hallucinations. The medical and psychiatric community almost universally regards non-ordinary experiences such as hearing voices, visions, tactile or olfactory hallucinations, as a sign of schizophrenia. The content or reality status of the experience is of no interest to the medical practitioner. Instead the therapeutic goal is to "normalize" the patient by eliminating the ego-alien intrusion. The dreadful side effects of powerful medications and the social stigma attached to the diagnosis have left many patients more isolated than ever from human community.

A tiny seed of change began in the Netherlands when a psychiatrist by the name of Marius Romme took an unprecedented step of shifting his focus from "voices-as-symptom" to simply "voices". In other words he took his patient seriously when she insisted that the only problem for her was the voices, not the schizophrenia. [76]

---

[74]   (Intervoice, 2012)
[75]   (Hearing Voices Network, 2012)
[76]   (Hornstein, 2009, p. 30)

Today there are flourishing groups for Voice Hearers (note the non-pejorative term) all over the world because of this new appraisal and attitude towards fictional voices. For example *Intervoice* aims to: [77]

- *show that hearing voices is a normal though unusual variation in human behaviour*
- *show that the problem is not hearing voices but the inability to cope with the experience*
- *educate society about the meaning of voices so as to reduce ignorance & anxiety and to ensure this innovatory approach on voice hearing is better known by voice hearers, families, professionals and the general public*
- *demonstrate the wide variety of voice hearing experiences and their origins, and peoples' approaches to coping*
- *increase the quality and quantity of mutual support available to all people and organisations involved in hearing voices work across the world*
- *make our work more effective and develop more non-medical ways of helping voice hearers cope with their experiences*

It seems that many people have such experiences today without being diagnosed at all. [78]

In a democratic gesture the *Hearing Voices Network* argues for meaning to emerge from the patient rather than imposing meaning (diagnosis) from outside experts. Once found, this meaning can be a life-long support and compass for the individual, helping them once again connect with others in a community.

Research into these non-ordinary states of mind is also going on in two broad fronts. Firstly, if the voices are not dismissed, but instead taken seriously, researchers are asking how a loving community can best support the individual in terms of functioning more adequately in his or her life; secondly, research is exploring the nature, causes, and origin of these voices.

---

[77]   (Intervoice, 2012)

[78]   (Hornstein, 2009, p. 32)

As far as the second goal of the research goes, a good deal of interest is going towards the connection between the appearance of voices and trauma, particularly sexual trauma. [79]

This approach seems to seek the aetiology of ego-alien mental states in actual traumatic events in the patient's life. Indeed many hearers seem to find solace in such explanations which do indeed tie disparate and disjointed life "happenings" into a tapestry of sorts that one can live with and indeed others (family, friends etc.) can live with too. Trauma is the going explanation for so many "clinical" conditions today that I would be hard pressed to enumerate them all but such an explanation at least does serve to bring one's "story" into alignment with the going narratives of today and that in itself is healing.

The fact that such explanations have this useful heuristic function does not mean that they are *true*! To get to *the* meaning or truth that lies deep within these strange experiences requires a method of research that stays absolutely faithful to the experiences and first hand narratives given by voice hearers and to enter those experiences deeply until the meaning is released. The Hearing Voices Network has begun this kind of research by the methodological stance of granting primacy to the actual experience of voices. But we need to go more deeply, rather than breaking off into sociological research (inquiries about actual past childhood experience etc.)

If we do this we enter a very strange arena indeed. First we pay attention to the staggering numbers of people who are emerging into the light, now that stigma is reduced, to claim their status as voice hearers. Next there is a universal claim among hearers that the voices are real, as concretely real as you or me speaking, and as sensual as another person's body (smells, tastes, visions, voices . . .) The voices have a kind of independence, autonomy, subjectivity, in a way similar to empirical reality. Yet most hearers would acknowledge that the voices are also the hearer's own mind. This objective reality occurring within the hearer's own mind cannot be collapsed into an identity with ordinary outer reality without the danger of psychosis.

---

[79]   Ibid

The two realities must thus be distinguished without reducing the reality status of *either* one! This distinction can be won for example by the hearer who challenges a voice to carry out a threat in outer reality (such as: "I can kill your parents"). When nothing happens, the hearer is in a position to *distinguish* the two realities, without devaluing either.

From this brief phenomenological investigation we are forced to articulate the following tentative meaning of the phenomenon of hearing voices today. I am advancing the hypothesis here, born out of the phenomenon of hearing voices itself, that:

A new reality is emerging into consciousness, catching more and more people up in its processes, particularly those who call themselves voice hearers. This reality:

- is "of the mind", yet objective, i.e. does not originate in the hearer's subjective mind;
- is "sensual", i.e., has a "body";
- has its own consciousness, which is not reducible to the hearer's subjective consciousness.
- is distinguishable from outer reality, but not spatially separate.
- Has the same reality status (convincing power) as empirical reality.

This is an exceedingly difficult and complex formulation of a new reality yet if we are to remain absolutely faithful to all aspects of voice hearers' experiences then we are forced to think this formulation.

Aspects of this new reality are manifesting more frequently today and are being dramatized in artistic forms such as performance or participatory art. It manifested in the man Jung "to the point of madness" and he worked very hard to comprehend the nature of his experiences, over a lifetime. My tentative formulation of some of the qualities of this new reality suggests that what is being aimed at by the soul is a manifest reality that is a unity of empirical and fictional realities, or more precisely, a unity of their difference.

The question arises if there could be a form of literature, or a form of writing, that may in effect be an act of tarning, a medium through which this possible future may manifest. This form would resemble *The Red Book* in that it would be *"writing autobiographical material but not as an autobiography."* However, it would have to avoid Jung's voluntary effort or project in which he positivized the fictional reality that was intruding into the ordinary, by privileging empirical reality, in accordance with the times he lived in. Instead, this "new genre" would have to be such that empirical reality and fictional reality would maintain their distinction while, at the same time, their unity would become apparent. It may be that the appropriate way to describe such a complex structure of consciousness is to say that a new form of selfhood is in formation and manifesting into actuality.

In what follows, I offer my own attempt at such a form of literature. The process involves memories of a dual consciousness, interweaving of past, present, and future, inner and outer reality, along with philosophical thoughts expressed in direct speech which emerged quite spontaneously. All these elements are brought to life in the adventures of the purely literary figures, David and Master John while the narrator is John, the author. Each character appears to lead a separate life but are they all really separate?

You will discover the truth at the very end.

TARNING AT WORK IN
A NEW FORM OF LITERATURE

SELF

Noun:

Inflected forms: pl. **selves**

1. *The total, essential, or particular being of a person; the individual*

2. *The essential qualities distinguishing one person from another; individuality:*

Etymology:

s(w)e-
Pronoun of the third person and reflexive (referring back to the subject of the sentence); further appearing in various forms referring to the social group as an entity, "(we our-)selves."

American Heritage Dictionary

WE OURSELVES

The question of whether individual actions can influence evolution! Yes, evolution is now a central aspect of the dialogue concerning our future as a species. This dialogue concerning evolution is split today! On the one hand we teach evolution as a mindless process of random mutations, a process that rolls on quite independently of individual input, and on the other we carry on political and economic debates in a tone of urgency that highlights the role of individuals in altering the course of our collective future at the level of survival of the species. We only have to think of terrorism, global warming, genetic engineering etc . . .

As we know, enormous power has fallen into the hands of individuals and many people and groups are morally alarmed and . . . (t)his has forced on us the following question: We have now arrived at a point in history where we must ask ourselves: how do we consider the role of individuals in the evolutionary process, theoretically and practically or, more precisely, how could individual action affect the course of our collective destiny?

If I am not mistaken, our future utterly depends on how we answer this question . . .

Master John Speaks:
Lesson I: Introduction to the Spiritual Problem of Our Times

Individual Effort

The spiritual journey so often begins with seeking. We sense something is wrong, missing and set out to seek . . . what: power, answers, wisdom, love, health? All this has a sense of adventure that can sustain us for quite a while. Things take quite a different turn when we discover the alarming fact that all the while, something has been seeking us . . .

Master John, *Aphorisms*

Another failure!

David muttered to himself as he left the interview. The question penetrated and now echoed in his brain like a drum: "With all your qualifications, why are you seeking a job as a Contract Counsellor? Why aren't you working as a Supervisor?" etc. The details didn't matter. The refrain was now very familiar. You ought to do a Ph. D, Why are you here working for $15 an hour? You have the experience to do X. Are you sure you want this job for the night time shift at a half way house? It only pays . . .

The trouble is when you go into an interview you end up sounding like your future employer's equal, or even superior! Why don't you tone it down? How? I can't! Even when you don't know, you sound like you do, you inflated bastard. Can't you be a bit more humble?

"Well, that's a new thought", David mused as he made his way to Starbucks for the cup of coffee that would sustain him for the empty hours that lay ahead that day. Like every bloody day it seems.

I wake up; write my dreams down, plunge into the day like everybody else, doing the right thing, being busy, looking for a job. I even paste the classifieds into an album so I don't lose track of the jobs I have applied for. I keep a list of phone calls made and to whom, whether I followed up, whether they returned my call. I am quite careful about these matters. I make sure that my papers are in order so that they can see I am qualified.

Why, then, can't I MAKE IT!

And so David's mantra went, expiring around 11 am. As his depression gained ground he gratefully slid back into bed "for a nap". That took care of the middle of the day when it was most painful to watch all the busy people being productive while his life was merely a waste. Around 2 pm, he regretfully woke up as usual and reached for his book, then down to the local café again, sitting with some frozen yoghurt while reading for the next couple of hours.

At last, everyone is coming home. It's 5 pm. There is nothing more to do today so no point in worrying about money, jobs, or even one's miserable life!

This was the high point of David's day: A time for discussion, movies, more reading, even a visit to friends.

These visits were strange though. While David enjoyed the company of others, he so often felt alien to their discussions. He joined in vigorously enough and even sometimes said things that others listened to, but there was a sense in him that his friends possessed something he definitely lacked. What *was* it? His friends discussed things he was very interested in but they were things related to what his friends were actually doing. But he wasn't! Even when he did join in and do things with others, like start up a co-operative, participate in community activities, join training groups and so on, he still felt, well, *alien*. It was as if in some fundamental way, he did not belong to any of it.

David could not help notice that his community of friends possessed a sense of *purpose*. They knew what they were doing each day. They discussed things as if they really mattered. They got up each day and went to work, or took initiative to start a campaign, or whatever . . . And whatever this *purpose* was, David definitely did not have it. At times in the middle of such conversations at night, David would suddenly feel as if he were looking down a telescope held the wrong way. He was here and everyone else was way down there, out of reach.

And he was very alone.

David never told anyone about this secret experience. He did not even admit it to himself. Rather, each evening he simply tried to connect again to others, until he got exhausted and once again slipped gratefully into bed.

Lying there awake, he began to notice small inexplicable events that worried him somewhat.

How come I seem to prefer breathing out to breathing in? When I breathe out, I lie there with no inclination towards breathing in again. I just lay here in complete stillness, until some far away impulse forces a breath in again.

And the cycle began again until sleep finally drew around him.

David also noticed that he vastly preferred going to bed to waking up in the morning. However, he loved waking up at around 1 am or so, as he often did. Everyone was asleep, except him. He tried not to wake up too much, but rather desired to stay in what he could only call the *in between place* as long as possible. It was here, in this place between worlds, that, for David, things really happened!

David had no purpose in keeping a dream journal. He had not been instructed about it nor had he been mentored into the value of staying "in between" waking and sleeping. He did not even know *why* he made those choices. He did not discuss the matter with anybody and was not wrapped up in any ideology about it. He simply desired to do those rituals and on this score his desire was for some unknown reason very strong. Put simply, he couldn't wait to go to bed at night in anticipation of what would surely follow: a dream that would startle him awake or a more subtle process that would leave him in an "in between" state where events occurred with as much reality as those that normally occur in our ordinary waking state.

Of course, the nature of these events was quite different from ordinary waking states.

Quite different . . .

We all agree we have our imagination today and we use what we "have" for any purpose that comes to mind. So the human imagination has degenerated into a mere tool for the lowest aspirations of ego. Truth has become a dirty word today and imagination as a vehicle for truth has probably now reached the status of a non sequitur. Psychology does not seek truth. Its goals are more immediate. It seeks evidence, i.e. evidence based research! Yet what counts as evidence? Here we see the modern scientific prejudice against any data that does not come through the "imagination-free" senses. In other words, positivism is working hard as usual. If I say I had a dream which says X, the only evidence the scientist can find is that I made a public claim. About what the dream actually says, no epistemological claim can be made whatsoever . . . and so Truth and her handmaiden retire to a cave to await better days . . .

Master John: *The State of Modern Psychology*

It's coming, again! It began softly, a whisper. David was lying on his back in bed, awake yet curiously powerless to move.

This time, don't panic! You can still breathe.

His senses were alive and his thinking intact in the sense that he knew where he was, i.e. in bed, yet he was simultaneously aware of being somewhere else. Not in the positivistic sense of being located somewhere else in space. Not at all! This "elsewhere" was right here as well.

Maybe it's always here and I have to get to it this way. Is it a WAY? I can't get to it wilfully. My will is actually diminished and another will is emerging and coming towards me.

The presence grew more strongly. Vibrations, an echoing sound with a definite beat, even wasps or bees. Louder and Louder, more insistent!

I am describing it as a sound but it does not belong to the senses. It's beginning to shake my body now. It's so strong, I must relax, let it in. Can I take it? Will I be shaken apart? A wave is breaking on me and I don't know if I can take it! A crescendo of beating . . . what: wings, insects, vibrations? What is happening to me?

And then it diminished, fading once more.

I've got to breathe, suck it in. Move!

David wrenched his will back from wherever it had been and rolled to his side. He was free again and awake to his surroundings but once again with a full memory of his experience. At first he felt a kind of triumph. This time he hadn't panicked and the vibrations hadn't killed him. He switched on his small desk lamp and reached for his journal, writing down from memory what had happened. He wrote quickly, before his memory became infused with associations that did not belong to the experience. Then he looked at his clock. Yes, 1 a.m. as usual. He felt tired. He *had* been penetrated. It was real. Something had really happened to him. There *is* a reality that he had entered and which had also entered him. There is a veil or a gate to that reality but it is not far away at all. Rather, this strange reality is near, co-extensive with ordinary reality. There is a key to that gate and it has to do with lowering the free will that we are each endowed with today. So far though, David could not enter voluntarily at all. These visitations came spontaneously in their own timing. The most David could do was to prepare himself each night for that possibility and to learn from each encounter. Tonight he had learned. He did not panic and wrench himself out of it too early as he had done before. He even remembered to stay calm while present in the *in between place*.

As he thought through the experience, recording in his journal as usual, his weariness increased and so he sank back into his bed, switching the light off. He slipped once again into sleep. He dreamed:

> *A man is among us, he looks quite normal, like the actor in Cocoon, except he is in fact alien. He is friendly, wants to, needs to live amongst us and is warmly welcomed. Many therapists are excited and thrilled with the glamour of his gifts, which include space ships that could fly at dizzying speeds. I join in with this madness for a bit but lose interest and instead grow increasingly alarmed.*
>
> *I try to warn others, saying, "What if . . . ? What if . . . ?" I decide to act. I want to burn him and race around looking for a flame thrower. Instead I kept grabbing fire extinguishers and spray him with those. They are useless. He tries to stop me and we seem to realize that there was nothing personal in this. He wants simply to live here and I could sense incredible danger to us. I say, "It's just that our species can't survive if you stay. We need to survive too!" Then I go back to my frantic search. He says, responding to my "What if . . ." s: "Do you mean, what if I spit on the carpet or people?" And he does so, thus at last revealing the danger. A terrible poison was in his spittle, it dissolves flesh leaving horrible forms, like a fly dissolves its meal. I get more frantic until . . .*
>
> *There is a bed of coals, so astoundingly hot that they each glow transparent red. One would simply evaporate on them. In the midst of my passion to stop the alien, a young man, a human,*

flings himself as a voluntary sacrifice onto the bed of coals. He is the sacrifice who will save us. I am struck with horror and agony, a religious agony that sends me to my knees as I feel his act of sacrifice. O God! O God O God! I imagine his flesh blackening and crisping as he rolls on the coals in unspeakable agony. Yet when I actually look, though I am screaming in pain and horror and awe, I can see quite objectively that he is undergoing a different process. He is moving about, but in agony or intentionally? That is, is he avoiding the heat or is he moving to further expose himself to it? He is not screaming. Is he in pain?

He then begins to glow red just like the coal itself. He becomes transparently glowing red all over, like a clay vessel does at the highest point that forms the pot. Even more astounding, he is pregnant, almost full term! Did he enter the ordeal that way or did the transforming fire engender a new life in him? By this time I cannot describe my own feelings at all. It's too much. One cannot name a mystery such as this.

He is our redeemer!

David woke up sharply, gasping with each breath. A strong smell of semen pervaded his nostrils though there was no physical release. It seemed to permeate his entire body. He wrote feverishly, recording as much detail as possible, although there was little chance of this experience fading from his memory.

I am exhausted and it's only 6 o'clock in the morning. This has gone on for years and it's getting more intense. I don't know how much more I can take.

Unable to sleep, filled with awe, David got up to make his customary cup of tea and toast. He checked his little son who was still sleeping peacefully, blessed in his innocence. It was a relief to see him there, a reminder of ordinary life.

I hope I am not leaning on him too much, David mused in some anguish, as he sipped his tea against the cold Seattle morning. His thoughts took a depressive turn:

Ordinary life! What's that? So many nights where I have these encounters that come through my body, followed by some dream in which my passions are aroused to full intensity with no release! Then within that dream I am given a vision that is objective in its quality. I am shown something true!

To make matters worse, the qualities of these encounters were emerging in David's waking life. The vibrations pervading his body were appearing as shudders during the day. It felt like a spring centred in his spine that would uncoil suddenly, forcing a shout from his belly. In his more sarcastic moments he wondered if he had developed some form of Tourette's. Furthermore David was assailed by a heat in his body that made him appear sunburned much of the time, complete with periodic shedding of his skin, like a snake. This heat was accompanied by an intense itching in his skin that he likened to a storm of insects peppering his face and like insects. It was relentless and impermeable to reason.

The psychological condition of ambiguity and ambivalence is the sine qua non *for an encounter with the spiritual realms. This is so because our modern structure of consciousness is founded on the either-or principle or the law of contradiction. We have achieved an acute self-consciousness through this principle and as a result have excluded or set ourselves apart from the root of our being, which we call the unconscious today. We therefore* know *nature but no longer participate* in *nature.*

The central question is: Did evolution intend this outcome and is it final?

Master John: *The State of Modern Psychology*

David's life was deteriorating. His symptoms were worsening and his hold on the ordinary world was weakening. He managed to find work as a therapist or educator in community centres and even maintained a small private practice. But he was now living in two worlds that seemed irreconcilable. During the day he earned a minimal living but the concerns of his colleagues were far removed from his own and the feeling of alienation increased. The sheer force of his encounters during the night was spilling into his daily life in alarming ways. During one job interview, he was asked what his plans for the future were. Some minutes into his grand exposition on the future of the world, David began to notice that his interviewer was looking aghast. He stopped. "What I mean is: do you plan to work here awhile or is this a temporary move for you?"

So it goes! As David left the interview, Vonnegut's wry phrase echoed in his mind yet again. *Another failure!*

He was getting worried now. He was beginning to feel like two worlds were colliding in him. As if to confirm this daunting feeling, another shudder uncoiled from his spine and a grunt forced itself from his throat. Looking nervously around, David could not help noticing that these sounds had a definite sexual tone to them. And he was physically hot again with the interminable itching which focused for some insane reason on his face, throat, and chest. He was turning red again, even tumescent. He quickly turned homeward ashamed to be seen in this obviously aroused state.

Perhaps if I relieve myself the usual way, it will calm down.

But that was part of the problem. David was experiencing yet another unbidden and certainly unwanted symptom. As sexual as his symptoms were, as obviously *phallic* as they appeared, he felt a peculiar injunction against relieving the pressure. It was more like an inhibition, in that his body refused to surrender to his will. He could arouse himself but there was to be no release. This of course dramatically increased the heat and pressure in David and his ability to function in the world, to be concerned with ordinary matters, declined even further.

He now could not open his mouth in public without the raw material of his nocturnal encounters bursting through into daylight, leaving him mortified with shame and drawing the most varied reactions from others around him.

For many years David had been a group leader, workshop leader, and educator. He was used to speaking to large numbers of people. But he was now losing control of his own speech centre. Others were attracted to or repelled by his words and synchronicities were beginning to constellate in the groups that he conducted. He could never predict an occurrence and he could never predict the outcome of an outburst. At times he sounded like a prophet, trumpeting the end of the world.

The speech that burst through in this manner was autonomous, hot blooded and imagistic. David had not integrated any of it into personal understanding and none of it could therefore be expressed in ordinary concepts. He even dreamed that blood was gushing out of his mouth: *Blood Speech!* During such speech, David felt elated, as if he were riding a wave of passion. This was invariably followed by a mortifying shame that suffused his whole body, igniting a flurry of self-criticism that would assail him for days afterwards. He felt a moral burden too.

How can I lead groups, run workshops, when I cannot predict what will come out of my mouth and worse, when I have no idea what the outcome will be? Some women are attracted to me for the wrong reasons, while others, men and women, are appalled by my words. I'm a loose cannon. Dangerous!

Armed with his newly found, desperate moral courage, David slowly withdrew from all public speaking, and his income rested solely on his small private practice. His self—incriminations, his desire to do the right thing, and his wish not to harm others, led to a feeling of self-righteousness about his "painful sacrifice". But there was no applause, only further reductions in income and further alienation from ordinary life.

David felt that his life was no longer his own. The alien nature of the autonomous speech disturbed and worried him. He was no longer master of his own house. In a way he was facing a double tragedy. His attempts to get on with his life, to succeed in *something* were clearly grinding to a halt. At the same time, he was not in control of his own body.

How many hours, days, and weeks do I have to spend in this damn basement, scratching my skin off, with heat pounding into me with no relief? I can't even get on a bus without a sudden plague of wasps attacking my head so that I have to use all my will to refrain from tearing my hair out! It's just not stopping! The bloody stupid emergency doctor prescribed steroids when I rolled up to the ward on New Year's Eve, my entire body looking like a red beacon!

No one can help me here!

Our species depends on a certain development taking place quickly but the base support for this development is very young. The evolutionary next step enters through the weakness in our personalities which are constructed to keep such changes out. In dreams this shows up as young persons, or animals, showing weakness and immaturity. A huge evolutionary process is taking place on a relatively weak base. Feelings of being too young, bearing too much responsibility, being abandoned by parents, are generated. The stakes are very high; the outcome very uncertain.

Master John Speaks: *Lesson IV: Intimations of the Future*

When David could get to sleep, it didn't stop there either. As the years went by, it became clearer to him that he was at the centre of incursions from two opposite directions. When he slipped into the *in between place* it felt like he was being infused with a *presence* that emerged from or, on the other hand, merged with his body. He was awake and could retain memory of the experience. He realized that he was facilitating this process by a lowering of his will and the more he could do this, the more intense the experience became. The state of consciousness that emerged is one where opposites begin to interpenetrate in a quite mysterious way to David. Meaning was always ambiguous which had the effect of taking him more deeply into the feeling of the experience. He even felt he was being initiated somehow by the experience itself, without the need for interpretation. The forms of the "other presence" were predominately *animal*.

One afternoon he was taking a nap on the couch and suddenly "woke up". The familiar paralysis was upon him again and to his amazement, he was nestling in the arms of a sleeping giant Brown Bear. The sheer *presence* of this animal was overpowering. It invaded every sense. David was intoxicated with the damp pungent odour of the bear; he could feel every coarse fibre of its hair; he felt the enormous weight of its paws across his shoulders; he touched the razor sharp claws that extended inches out and which could rake his flesh with ease. It was *real* and yet David knew he was in the *in between place* where his consciousness was now interpenetrating with the bear's. He wanted to flee but instead lay quietly until his normal consciousness returned. He knew that from now on he would have to take the bear into account with every choice he made. The bear was behind and around him and he was no longer alone.

On another occasion, after spending a social afternoon with a young woman, David returned home with tremendous heat once again racing through his body. Exhausted, he lay down and then:

> *I am in bed aware that I am sleeping, yet awake. I feel*
> *something entering that feels dangerous. I feel the presence of*
> *an animal merging with me, co-extensive with my human*
> *form. I move into a crouch position on the bed. I feel rippling*
> *power arcing through my chest and my mouth elongates and*

my teeth are sharp and bared. A growl utters easily from my chest. Power and grace in the animal body yet I am still human, too. I am conscious of my human experience while at the same time I have entered an animal consciousness. The power I feel is exhilarating. I have never felt such freedom. It takes over my speech centres and growls a long basso note with consummate ease. In fact he enters my entire body. All my senses are now available to him.

Over time, David had similar experiences with different animal figures. In each case the gateway to the experience lay in a surrender of will, leading to a kind of paralysis and at the same time a new kind of consciousness in which David became a figure amongst other figures all with the extraordinary capacity to interpenetrate one another. At the same time it was clear that David possessed something unique which attracted the other figures, i.e., a sensory-nervous system. It was hard to avoid the conclusion that he was being asked to "stand aside" for these animal figures so they could enter his sensory-nervous system in a manifestation process. Some were less pleasant than others and carried great warning . . .

. . . the serpent rises in me. I become him and I feel his head co-extensive with my own, my senses are being used by him. I slither downstairs to the large group below; I can feel a deep inhuman look has taken me over. The snake rises up in the middle of the room and surveys the people. Will it strike or not? They seem to know about it. I/the snake go in a circle and then leave the room. I then return to myself and collapse on the floor. A young woman comes over. I need/love her. She has the snake quality too. We look at the floor. Deep burns in the floor from its scales. They say in a kindly way that I must explore this somewhere else as the house is getting ruined.

In another scene I/the snake sprays poison all over the wall ruining the wall paper.

I wake up feeling cold with fear in the belly and a deep love for that young woman. The people wanted the serpent to strike someone in the group but I refused. I could do so apparently.

> *I am being subject to the will of another. It is inexorable and encompasses my circle of knowledge. I am an object of its knowledge and I cannot grasp its intentions.*

David had similar experiences with the lion, panther, elephant, butterfly, and eagle but the majority was with the cobra. He was exhilarated, shaken, in awe, elated and frightened by the extent and magnitude of what was happening to him. But what WAS happening to him? There was nothing in the contemporary world picture that could remotely address these profound experiences. And so David's acute sense of alienation deepened along with a feeling of being privileged, special, or singled out.

He cast a wide net out into literature, philosophy, mythology, depth psychology, and biology, seeking some companionship, and some understanding as well. It became clear that whatever he found in the literature, he was going through an initiatory process *by the figures themselves*. He knew enough about ritual to understand that initiation involved ordeals or direct experience of a spiritual reality, along with relevant instruction from an elder. David was receiving both from his experiences. One night:

> *I am in a yard, sitting in a lotus position facing the setting sun. I feel warm and comfortable, expectant. I had previously given all my money to the aboriginals. Now a big, strong, man comes (the actor George Kennedy). He looks strong and capable, a man who handles wild animals easily. His role here is to be a Snake Handler. He deftly stretches my arms above my head and then pulls me firmly over on my belly, still in the lotus. I feel hot. Two dogs are sniffing around me, excited, barking. I feel helpless, excited, wanting it to happen. It does. The serpent once again rises up my spine to head level. The Handler expertly puts his foot firmly in the small of my back as if I am the snake. And indeed I/it am frothing at the mouth and deep hisses coming from deep in my/its belly. I/it twist to bite him. The Handler deftly gets out of the way. Someone remarks that if the serpent wins, Watch Out! The Handler replies, "Then it will be a winner in the world somewhere, no matter the outcome here." I can also feel the serpent as if he is coiled next to my left hand*

> *outside my body. I feel glad, smiling (the smile of the possessed)*
> *all the time. I/he am twisting, hissing, striking venomously*
> *under the handler's foot. There is a fear from the spectators that*
> *the serpent will overcome me. The Handler is trying to help me*
> *and seemed to want the serpent to rise, which it did. I could not*
> *do it alone.*

Slowly, David began to tease out some aspects of his ordeal that he could work with. First of all it became clear to him that his ordeal was related to the accounts of shamanic initiations with their close affinity with the animal realm. Shamans had the capacity to speak for the animal world, to align their people with animal wisdom in order that the community did not stray too far from it. The shamanic initiation had to do with undergoing extreme ordeals for the purpose of overcoming our fear of death. Only then can the shaman call up the powers of nature for purposes of healing or education.

The prevalence of the cobra and its association with the spinal column in David's encounters led him to the Kundalini system of India. He immersed himself in autobiographical accounts of individuals who had undergone spontaneous eruptions of Kundalini energies. He learned that this was happening frequently in the West in modern times. It was almost always disturbing and disorienting, often leading to psychological difficulties for the individuals caught up in the fiery energy.

David discovered how these two psychological systems of shamanism and Kundalini were steeped in ancient wisdom, profound and vast. However, he became disturbed by the fact that most other modern individuals who underwent their version of initiation ended up by assimilating their own experience to the system of ancient thought that was already in place, bequeathed to us from our ancestors. This led to an industry of modern shamanic or Kundalini healing practices.

Although David longed to bring his experiences into the world, to make money, to contribute and most of all to bring to a close his appalling sense of isolation, he felt strangely repelled by the thought of these ancient forms being resuscitated and imitated by modern people who in fact had little to do with actual animals or ancient yogic practices. The fact is, these ancient forms are now obsolete. They do not and cannot contribute to the contemporary world picture in their original forms. From the outside, to modern consciousness, such practices simply look anachronistic and well, weird! And David was not prepared to ignore the contemporary world picture, with all its modern problems that the past alone cannot possibly adequately address.

These considerations simply made David more miserable, with a deepening sense of not belonging anywhere, the past or the present. Well, perhaps that leaves the future. Was it possible that in some way he belonged to the future? This thought came as something like a revelation to David. As if in support for such a thought, David's experiences in the *in between place* took another turn and sent him off in another line of inquiry altogether.

He encountered figures that were of human form!

One night:

> *I am in bed and I am dreaming of a woman who is inside of me skin to skin. She is beginning to separate from me and is kissing me from the inside, making love to me. I am aroused but also scared too. It feels uncanny to have someone in my skin, sharing my body. I begin turning to see her. I want to see her but she resists me. It's like one body moving to two separate wills. I get scared but I manage to turn around expecting to see a witch. I see a young woman. I look into her eyes deeply and I see the universe of stars. I keep thinking of the Knights Templar. I don't think she wants me to look at her. I feel possessed. I am aware that I am dreaming. She comes out of my skin again and holds me down. It's like she is a little behind me. I can physically feel her arms and body. I turn around again and our mouths meet. Hers is like honey. She resists at first but her moistures are flowing. I touch her and we begin to make love. I feel both of us as we move together. She is distinguishable from me yet she came out of me.*

There was no mistaking the nature of *this* experience. David knew it belonged to mystic traditions where an initiate discovers the "woman within", his soul, and the one who would instruct him in the mystery of Love. Yet this was only the beginning for David. Several years later, as his separation from the community deepened inexorably, he finally moved out of his home, leaving his wife and son. It was not his choice. His wife had gradually come to the conclusion that she simply could not get on with her own life as long as David was there. It was true! His almost mad ravings about nocturnal encounters with invisible beings or accounts of visions of the future of the world were dominating the household, not to mention his fiery symptoms that almost drove him to desperate measures at times, day in, and day out, for years. The process was relentless and she had had enough!

It's easy, perhaps inevitable that we feel privileged or special when the spirit draws near. And this is an important feeling that brings balance. It balances first, a tendency in the West to adopt ancient Eastern ideas and to think that the spiritual task involves loss of one's individuality in "the ocean of bliss". And secondly it balances a sustained and pervasive feeling that one is "only a worm", to be used and perhaps broken by the awesome Power that enters the human experience. One can oscillate between these extremes for some time.

Master John Speaks: *Lesson X: The Manifestation Process*

It was as if something intended David's awful isolation in order to prepare him for what was to come next. The very next day, when he had settled in his rented room at a friend's house, it started to happen. David began to experience ecstasy. He only had to retire to his room and quieten his mind down and a glorious fountain of fluid would pervade his entire body. During the following weeks his body was flooded with a kind of nectar that produced an ecstasy in him. He could smell flowers or sweet fragrance in the air. He felt he had grown a pair of wings, palpably, concretely. The erotic intensity was such that he would lay down for hours as a fount of glorious liquid fire poured into him. Many dreams came, and visions. The flood swept away everything that he had so far assumed about life, the human condition and its limitations. He was given experiences of a concrete nature, whose reality could not be questioned at all and yet which could not possibly be reduced or interpreted back into known categories of experience.

At the peak of his ecstasies, he met a being who he called his Beloved Star Sister. She came to him while he was fully awake, alone in his bed. He could get out of bed and see quite clearly with his outer vision that he was alone, yet he also saw, felt, and touched her there beside him, as real as his knowledge that he was alone. Both realities were interpenetrating each other. It was then that he experienced himself as being loved by another, totally, as an object of divine desire. Here he learned that the human body is able to receive an influx of love from the beyond. The heart is the door and it is the self-imposed limitations of the ego that close the door. He felt fearful that he could not contain it and was told again and again by his divine lover that he could, that he needed only to open up completely, right to the level of the cells of his body. He discovered that he could do this, and that in that condition of complete surrender, he received the poetry that later came to him.

His "poems" were really a *poesis*, a making. David expressed and described what was happening within and to him while it was occurring. Something was forming in him and he was transforming at the same time. He was being initiated into the profound mystery of love, directly by love itself. The *quality* of the initiation was this: David's desires were fully aroused. He was deeply immersed in an ocean of pleasure and from within that intoxicating brew, he received specific spiritual instructions about how to be a creature of love. That is, David was to remain conscious and not sink into blissful oblivion. His task was to remain objective within the field of desire so that he could perceive spiritual reality and then remember what he had perceived.

What can we say about the modern spiritual task? It's clear that we all feel the spiritual wasteland that is so stunningly upon us. Many are choosing to go to sleep and entire industries are built around that choice. Others seek out established traditions and become practitioners of ancient wisdom. Others are moving towards new forms of religion that attempt to address modern circumstances. So we see groups claiming that God and Money are not antagonists after all but in seeking money one is doing God's Will etc. None of these seem to me to address the pivotal psychological fact of this modern life: that we are each endowed with a free and unique self which has separated from its spiritual roots. Surely the modern spiritual task must take this fact into account. The answer lies not in losing that hard won freedom but rather to find a way to reunite with our common source in freedom.

Master John: *Commentaries*

David's experiences with animal wisdom led him into many fields of inquiry. He was not a scholar but rather was attempting to stave off his crippling isolation by finding companionship in literature. Similarly his encounters with love led him into a study of poetry, the Renaissance, medieval courtly love, depth psychology, romanticism, romantic theology and of course mystical autobiography. He also dived into sophianic philosophy that had emerged in Russia. All these efforts were guided by his dreams. It was not a systematic endeavour designed to gain mastery over this or that field. He was drawn to any account of a human love that was unconsummated in the usual way. He studied the consequences of such a love in terms of cultural transformation. The psychology of such transformations included the arousal of passions that were outwardly denied but not suppressed. They were instead intensified as a preparation for entering those spiritual realms that are in fact the seed bed of all future cultural forms. Those realms seemed to have exactly the same qualities that David experienced in his *in between place* and in his dream-visions.

At the same time, David still asked the same question as with his "shamanic" and "kundalini" experiences. Were his encounters with the beloved another instance of the past? The overlap with the experience of others in the past was uncanny. He fastened on Dante in particular. David too had suffered an unrequited love when he was young and that love was the engine to his creating a new kind of school, at the age of twenty-three. Although the school did not last, he was changed forever, and his young love kept appearing to him in dreams for the next thirty nine years, always as a lover, mentor, guide and initiatrix.

If the meaning of these encounters was the creation of a new cultural form, then David once again was placed in the future, neither belonging to the past or the present. He felt some comfort with this thought. And it seemed to help him make sense of the fact that every structure in his own life was coming apart. It just would not stop. Career, marriage, family, home, all disappeared. Then his personality structure underwent a melt-down. David was being stripped down to the core. All that he had habitually thought about, i.e., the three great relationships: man and god; man and nature; man and man was melted down under the impact of his inner encounters.

The question, when it arrived in his consciousness, became the driving force to his life, the thread to the future and at times, the slim hope that he was after all still sane.

What then, is the new form?

So, what do I mean by form, or image? It's simply the way we regard self, others or nature. I don't mean the way we may consciously think about ourselves etc. I mean how we perceive without thinking about it: our common sense, in other words. This is another way of saying: reality. *The way we customarily regard the world is reality. Why do I bother using a possibly misleading word like* form? *Why not just say reality? Well, the remarkable thing is: we can sometimes trace the genesis of what we call real to the efforts of a single individual whose discovery in the realm of thought is taken up by others and gradually everyone's perceptions are extended by that creative thought. Soon, the thought is forgotten and only the perception remains, not as a perception per se, but as a common sense fact, i.e., reality.*

Well, these creative individuals were definitely confronted with forms or images.

Master John Speaks: *Questions and Answers*

David's encounters with images as animal powers interpenetrating with his sensory-nervous system were not to be understood as preparing him for a career as a modern shaman. He was clear about that error. But he clearly was being prepared in the manner of an initiation. Entering the *in between place* and finding these beings who seemed to seek him out, all had the character of a fully sensual experience. David could not avoid feeling that he was meant to *become* these animal images, to allow them to enter him without interpretation. He felt that the experiences themselves would change him.

Over time he noticed that his mind was settling down while his senses were sharpening. His skin, in particular was becoming an organ of sensation that responded to very small stimuli. A hair brushing his skin felt delicious whereas a twig snapping back on an arm was unbearable. If David became stressed or was present to conflict, he often heated up and his skin broke out in painful itching again. He had to find ways to lower the effects of light and sound on him. He also underwent a radical change in diet. This transformation taking place in his physiology seemed to be strengthening him.

But for many years David was not sure at all whether he would physically make it. The extent and magnitude of his inner encounters were exhausting him and for some mad reason he kept showing up for more. The precariousness of his condition became clear when one night he dreamed:

> *I am on a winding road in the country. I see a young woman throwing a boomerang in a field. It comes my way. I pick it up and throw it. This attracts her and she comes my way and joins me. We go by some animals and see a calf split off from the herd. The calf is plaintively bleating for its mother but it is now alone. In the long grass lies a huge golden cobra. As the calf nears, the cobra rears up and glides easily onto the calf's back. There, it curls up on its new home. Astonished, the calf ceases bleating as it can barely take the weight of the Golden One and can do no more than try not to collapse. I watch in great trepidation. I do not know the outcome.*

David had read how many people called to a spiritual task describe such a burden. Embodying a new spiritual truth or developing new spiritual capacity always involves the body. Our material reality confers limitations on the spirit which is free in its immaterial state. And the human being pays the price of this limitation. David had devoured these accounts and for a long time did not know whether he would simply count as a small part of the human wreckage down through history as the spirit worked out its and our destiny on earth. There was a frightening impersonal quality to the process that David was undergoing. He sensed that if the calf's back broke, if his physiological base could not sustain the burden of his task, then the cobra would simply find some other candidate. Qualifications for candidature include isolation from the community, and a weakness in the personality. David's weakness lay in his attitude towards the animal body. He undervalued it. Sexuality, the passions, and desire had played a large part in David's life but always with a subtle devaluation. David liked *to know* and any experience that took him from his understanding of things was felt to be a regrettable failure, a temporary loss of control to be answered by extra efforts *to know* what was going on.

So his initiation into animal wisdom carried with it an element of horror. David realized that he had been given a task simply because he was available through his own incompleteness and not because he was special, with special powers etc. The objective fact that human beings are broken, not as punishment, not because nature is cruel but because it is *just so*, horrified him. David stared into the abyss and recoiled! Human morality was nowhere to be seen.

Struggling to understand at least something within the majesty of being that he was now exposed to, David wondered if there was something terribly important to the process of completing the man as a prelude to receiving the spirit.

We have developed a civilization that is too one-sided. Look at me for god's sake. I was born into a time where survival depends only on having an intellect. We educate children, not to be whole but to emphasize only one or two capacities of the mind, to the point that if you can't do these things (the 3 R's) you are called learning disabled. All traditional initiation practices are finished now, and they were centrally concerned with creating a more whole being, i.e. a being that included the animal-spiritual life.

All that I believed in, everything that supported me in this modern life has been stripped away—and look at me! Most of my time down here in the bloody basement, howling in pain, or feverishly writing in my journal as if my life depends on it! I can't wait for the next dream and I can't stand what I am seeing in them. Yes, my one-sidedness is being corrected by these experiences but I am getting disabled from functioning in the world as a result.

What's the bloody point of becoming more complete if I can't function!

David's depression deepened to the point of suicide. He could not find a criterion for continuing or ending it. His love for his son kept him going to be sure but on what basis could David choose life when he was being shown how one-sided, how dangerously one-sided our lives were becoming? As well as being inducted into the animal spirit, a realm of sensuality, where the body and its ancient wisdom prevailed, David was also shown through a peculiar kind of vision what the *meaning* of our present one-sided culture is. And he was shown relentlessly. The more he opened up, the more was shown to him. The more he came to accept his weakness, the more complete he became and the more he was able to hold, within consciousness, the visions that came to him. And they came in a peculiar *form*. David came to realize that this form itself, as much as the dream content *is the actual cure to our one-sidedness* and holds the key to our future! One night:

> *I am working at a thermonuclear facility along with others. It is the central facility of our society. It is regulated and master-minded by a central computer, much like HAL in '2001', even to the detail of the red eye with which we could communicate. This computer is female. Everybody thought of her as an IT! In contrast I would look into her eye and talk to HER, subject to subject, with love. In other words, the feminine regulating principle which is the glue of society, by relating all parts to one another and to the whole, has become an IT!*

But my response alone is not enough. Slowly the lack of relatedness begins to drive her mad with grief. At first, this madness showed up as an increasing, dangerous autonomy in the operation of the objects associated with the facility (society)—elevators going sideways, doors opening and shutting autonomously, etc. Then people began to harm one another in various ways until the social system became frayed and anarchy increased, with civilization and its values losing cohesion and crumbling.

I now find myself in a garbage dump, near the central facility. Some abandoned children gave me a gun to kill them. I take it away from them. A vagabond is sitting in an abandoned car, sewing a boot for the coming (nuclear?) winter. He also used to work in the facility, he said. A sick woman careens by. A man tries to take his twin boys up a tower.

Then I am standing at the centre of the facility. It is Ground Zero. A large cleared area of gray sand and dirt with concentric rings, like a target, radiating from the centre. The ground is slightly raised at the centre, like a discus, sloping away to the edges. I sense that she is going to explode. I am right at the epicentre. She is going to destroy us all, and this means herself, in an apocalypse of rage, despair, loathing, hate, and grief, because of our stupidity. I must get away from the epicentre now. I sprint across the field, down the slight incline to the periphery of the field and sprawl prone, with my head facing the centre, just as she explodes.

The wind starts from the centre and blows out (in contrast to the natural phenomenon which sucks up). It begins as a breeze, increasing in strength and intensity until it becomes an unbearable shriek. Lying face down, I am sheltered by the slope as the wind rips over my back. But I mustn't raise my head at all—a few inches of protection and that's it! Then I know the shriek is hers. I "see" her standing at the centre, and a poem bursts spontaneously out of me as I record the experience:

> *The Goddess,*
> *Flowing*
> *In Her Agony.*
> *Awesome!*
> *Incomparable Grief and Rage*
> *Divine Suffering*
> *Excruciating Pain*
> *Such Terrible Agony*
> *Beauty, Sublime Beauty*
>
> *How is Love possible?*
> *Yet this is what I feel.*

A bubble of calm forms around me while the storm of destruction rages on outside. She is with me in a form that I can talk to, personally . . . Then the bubble collapses and the wind/goddess shrieks again. Gradually it dissipates and as I turn over, feeling its last tendrils whip at my clothes, I find myself tumbling out of this apocalyptic scene into a city street, the everyday world of my daily life. I have been returned from a visionary place to my ordinary life.

Then, I wake up.

David was badly shaken and at the same time exhilarated. He decided to call it a dream-vision because of its peculiar structure. He was asleep and yet within the dream he was awake in the same way as he normally is awake, i.e. experiencing himself as a self-aware being while perceiving objectively in the ordinary way. But what did he perceive in the ordinary way? A vision of extraordinary power confronted him, a vision in which he was *participating*, no longer an observer in the ordinary way!

David had studied our one-sidedness today in all aspects of our lives, and how it finds its root in the kind of consciousness we all have. Our modern consciousness is an either-or style of consciousness, often called Cartesian consciousness. The subjective-objective split is foundational to all other splits we suffer from. At bottom we experience our inner lives as *subjective* while our outer sense-bound lives are *objective*. Our knowledge system is based on this either-or stance.

He read how the growth of this knowledge system meant that our own human imagination for example can never be an organ through which we gain knowledge of the outer world. Even the Romantics had repudiated its truth value, while extolling its beauty. The imagination reveals only our inner subjective states. Knowledge of the world we live in only has one champion: science and its methodology.

Our modern form of consciousness therefore has led us into extreme one-sidedness in all three foundational aspects of our lives: man *or* god, man *or* nature, self *or* other. The effect spreads out into all our human activities and endeavours, as is readily observable in the growing number of accounts of an impending crisis in the world.

David had read many of these explanations of our current crisis and even embarked on a doctoral program in order to formalize his learning in this area. He decided to research his own experiences, calling his thesis: *The End of the World as a Crisis in Consciousness*. He of course was referring also to his own crisis which was deepening.

His dream-vision, and others like it, were showing David both the nature of the crisis as understood by the soul, and its transformation. When the being of the *other* is subjected to the either-or split and treated as an "it", the vision shows the apocalyptic result. At the same time, David was shown what lies on the other side *if* we each can endure the consequences of our own actions! Love may be born out of the violence of grief, rage, and destruction.

David's dream-vision, also presented the psychological structure of the redeeming consciousness. This structure overcomes and transforms the present either-or consciousness in that the life destroying split between subjective and objective is finally overcome. Furthermore the new structure is intimately connected with love. It may be, David mused, that love can only enter the human experience through this new structure of consciousness.

David was stymied. How to articulate this new structure in a way that does not fall back into our present either-or consciousness! It would have to sound like a contradiction. He nonetheless tried in his doctoral thesis to say something:

> . . . *this thesis presents the hypothesis that the end of the world can be experienced as an objective reality within the subjective life of an individual. This hypothesis is an attempt to resolve the split between an "inner" interpretation and an "outer" one by presenting the possibility that individuals may personally experience the objective reality of the end of the world . . .*

He was fortunate enough to find a few companions in the literature who had formulated something similar: Owen Barfield was one:

> *We have to distinguish between subject and object, not just in the field of commonplace experience, where "object" means matter and "subject" means ourselves. We have to distinguish between subjective spirit and objective spirit, or between spiritual experience that is merely subjective and that which is also objective, or between that which is merely ourselves and that which is another being in ourselves.*

David realized in a kind of epiphany that he had discovered the new form. It was a kind of double vision in contrast to modern consciousness which is a single vision. With this double vision one could simultaneously perceive ordinary reality but at the same time ordinary objects may be perceived as images of a spiritual reality that is objective, quite different from projective dynamics which display only subjective qualities.

This is also quite different from belief. Many of us now *believe* we are interconnected, for example. But we do not perceive it. So we continue to treat one another as objects. With the new structure of consciousness, we can *perceive* it as direct experience. This, David intuited, is where the future lies.

If David belonged to the future then this was it! This is the future form of consciousness that is emerging into the human domain. It appeared to be happening to him! He had been shaped by the molten heat of his inner encounters as preparation to receiving this great gift of cosmic love.

He felt that he had been given a task, and at the same time was free to refuse it. He was shown *what is*, with no moral imperative to act unless it came from within him. So many of the encounters he had with spiritual reality had to do with using his senses and in particular, his speech centre.

I am being made into a mouthpiece!

David had long felt the initiatory quality of his encounters with spiritual beings and this was the aim, the purpose, to create a mouthpiece for the love that can only incarnate through the new structure of consciousness.

David decided to create a name for this consciousness. He called it *participatory consciousness*.

The great insights David gained over a relatively short time as he was preparing for his doctoral program had a heavy cost. He decided to accept anti-anxiety medication for a few months so that he could cope with his academic program. He suffered panic attacks that immobilized him for hours at a time. He had little money and went into credit card debt, eventually declining into a personal bankruptcy. His body, like the calf, was groaning under the weight of his spiritual burden. In contrast the spirit, having found a willing host, kept pouring in.

What does it take today to overcome the spirit-matter split so deeply embedded in our present structure of consciousness? First and foremost it takes the moral courage to deny any further acting out of that split and to face it within oneself. This creates a condition of utter loneliness, a feeling of being separate from just about everything. But if you can hold that split in consciousness then you can expect eventually to find an advocate, a companion who is by your side and who can guide you towards the future.

Master John: *The State of Modern Psychology*

Under the dual weight of the demands from the spirit and his escalating impoverishment in the material realm, David finally entered his version of the *Dark Night of the Soul,* or to put it another way, he ascended the Cross. He felt utterly abandoned by the community and equally abandoned by any spiritual advocate. His existential condition broke in on him one day while driving down the freeway. He suddenly realized how much he had lost. While others were living their lives with at least some degree of success, helping life continue in some way, he in contrast had lost years of achievement. His was a life based on massive failures.

For God's sake, here I am living in one of the most beautiful States in the USA and I have barely gone beyond the boundaries of my own backyard, or basement. I haven't taken my son anywhere; my professional colleagues are prospering, my friend invites me to his family Christmas's because he knows I have no family; I have no money, no investments . . .

In the middle of the freeway he broke into a wail that held back nothing. Accumulated grief and rage swept through him and at the same time he had to stay aware of his surroundings, driving down a freeway at sixty miles per hour. Suicide was now a real and viable alternative for him. There was nothing to hang onto from the past and there was nothing to look forward to in the future.

Deep within such passions assailing the personality, like storm waves that batter the walls of a fortress, there may be discovered an island of utter and complete calm. David found his way to this island. He drove home and calmly picked up the old shotgun that he kept, along with the shells he had bought. He once again got into his car and drove eastward into the country. He had no plan. He simply drove, following the road, turning whenever necessary, not in a hurry. The sun was setting and it was a cold winter's day. He turned off the main road and strangely found himself being steered towards an isolated road marked "Dead End"!

Perfect!

He did not say the words of his intended action. He was simply in a place of great calmness, a place of silence. He got out of the car and walked around to the boot where the gun was packed away. As he reached for the gun, he glanced down on the road and there at his feet was a dead heron, frozen. He was stunned! David knew enough to recognize a synchronicity when he saw one. The heron is a pre-eminent symbol of the world soul and in a flash David knew he was acting out her suffering. He was feeling not only his own pain but hers as well.

I am not alone. I have found my advocate!

He gently lifted the body into his car and drove slowly and thoughtfully home. It was dark when he arrived and so he left the body in the car and went inside. On an intuition, he went to his library and pulled out a book by C.S. Lewis. It was *Perelandra*, the second book in a trilogy. He opened to a page and read the following passage: [80]

> *The thing still seemed impossible . . . he had not thought but known that, being what he was, he was psychologically incapable of doing it; and then without any apparent movement of the will, as objective and unemotional as the reading of a dial, there had arisen before him, with perfect certitude, the knowledge 'about this time tomorrow you will have done the impossible' . . . His fear, his shame, his love, all his arguments, were not altered in the least . . . he might beg, weep, or rebel—might curse or adore—sing like a martyr or blaspheme like a devil. It made not the slightest difference. The thing was going to be done . . . the whole struggle was over, and yet there seemed to be no moment of victory. You might say that the power of choice had been simply set aside and an inflexible destiny substituted for it. On the other hand, you might say that he had been delivered from the rhetoric of his passions and had emerged into unassailable freedom. Ransom could not, for the life of him, see any difference between these two statements. Predestination and freedom were apparently identical.*

David had long felt Lewis as a spiritual companion and now he knew him as a spiritual advocate! He understood where he, like the fictional

---

[80]   (Lewis, 1943, p. 184)

Ransom, had arrived: in perfect freedom to choose his destiny. There *was* no difference!

Over long years of isolation, David had been battered and shaped like a metallurgist beating on hot metal. He had been prepared by initiatory experiences to receive, become, and then to speak from the new form of consciousness that still belonged to the future.

David was to become a mouthpiece of the future!

Community of Souls

Alienation and isolation are necessary conditions for the spiritual seeker. Even though the great religions stress the importance of the spiritual community or sangha, there always comes a time to leave these umbrellas and strike off on one's own.

There is terrible danger in this. Banishment has always been the cruellest form of punishment, often resulting in death, or as they once said, loss of soul. Even today in modern prisons we remember enough of the ancient ways to know how to punish prisoners most harshly with solitary confinement, white walls, and a single bright unwavering light above.

The human soul prospers in community and withers in isolation, though the spirit may soar. This raises the question of how can the human soul possibly prosper when the initiate leaves the company of his fellows and enters the desert.

I think it is crucial to remember that the community of souls does not limit itself to embodied souls. There is also a community of souls who have previously been embodied and have left their legacy in earthly works. Such works can become the gateway to a communion with these souls, bringing real comfort and solace to the seeker. The literal past is not inaccessible to experience at all—the psychological past is. Our ancestors are right here, ready to commune with the living and to express their concerns.

And there are others whose paths do not include earthly existence at all, yet who are also vitally concerned with the outcome of our existence, individually and as a species.

Master John Speaks: *Lesson VII: Perils of the Soul*

It was 3 pm Sunday 14th December, 1997. David had to be exact. Several people were flying in from around the country at this time to discuss his doctoral program. He had created a document which outlined the course of his studies for the next few years, culminating in a proposed thesis on the evolution of consciousness.

This was David's greatest hope for regaining a connection with the community, after so many years "in the spirit". He had been given some great spiritual treasures but the task of bringing that gold back into ordinary life still lay ahead. So, he was terrified. This was his first attempt to make his efforts intelligible to other, discerning academics. He had deliberately chosen some who were unfamiliar with his chosen field of Consciousness Studies. One was a journalist, while his Reader, the most important member who stayed in the background, never attending the meetings, held a Ph.D. in Education. David had to be sure that he could reach into the non-specialised community of scholars, and beyond.

Crafting the Learning Agreement was an exercise in agony. For years David had been expanded, with creative images and thinking pouring into him. He had written copious notes of his experiences, while they were happening to him and shaping him at the same time. These notes comprised the "data" for his thesis. Converting these to a more prosaic form suitable to an academic degree physically hurt David. He was required to contract, become denser, and in doing so, his body heated up like a lamp. Writing was a channel for that energy, like a heat sink. If he stopped, the energy had nowhere to go and his physical body paid the price with fiery symptoms that incapacitated him. The most dangerous symptom was a strong smell of electricity in his nose. A clear warning sign to act! And so he wrote furiously. There was no shortage of material. The problem was how to condense it into a finite document that spelled out the steps in his doctoral program.

He needed help with concepts and methodologies that were already available but he also needed a different *kind* of help. Literature reviews in doctoral programs help the student "locate himself" somewhere in scholarship. From this launch pad, he can extend knowledge in a certain field or more rarely, he can make an original contribution to scholarship.

David needed to do this too, of course. The Learning Agreement he was about to present to his committee on this particular Sunday had to be very specific on this score.

David needed, more than anything else, a hint in the literature that others had journeyed to the same realm as David had or at least had intuited its existence and qualities. He was reading, not only to gain concepts but to sniff out a trail back to the author's soul. If he was successful he could then commune with that soul and receive not dead concepts but the fruit of the author's own labours in life. This would be a gift to him and the bridge back to the living community. It was the difference between using an author's concepts for David's own purposes and having those concepts breathed into him from the author himself. David's own voice would then be expressing that soul's concerns as well as his own, advancing them into the new context.

More specifically, David ardently wished for a community of souls who had at least intuited the existence of the world forming out of the future in the soul of humankind—the same world that he had discovered himself through his new personality structure, the structure that wisdom intended for that purpose. This community, if it existed, would comprise souls who were contemporaneous with David within a few hundred years at most. This was because an intimate knowledge of the structure of modern consciousness was a necessary condition for intuiting or experiencing the new structure that would emerge from and transform the old one. As important as *this* requirement was for David, an understanding of evolution was also vital for his own work and thus for the choice of his community of souls.

When an unsuspecting individual is inundated with spiritual energies that undo everything that the person has believed about self and life in general, the razor's edge between madness and initiation is comprised of *meaning*. Can the initiate find or discover the underlying meaning to the wild turbulence that assails the soul? David had the capacity to perceive and contain images of the soul that expressed the spiritual meaning. Thus he was able to perceive the two-fold structure of his own vision-dreams in which he both observed and participated in extraordinary events. He could therefore slowly come to understand that a new world was emerging from within the ordinary modern world and that it needed human participation to become a reality.

A transformation in both human being and world was in the making!

David was sure this process is emerging from the future. He was sure because his own experiences could not be understood solely in terms of his own personal past. The images that came to him were sufficiently strange that he had to take them in their own terms. So his language became more tensile in an attempt to express the concepts that lay within the images.

A process emerging from the future! Such thoughts were exceedingly strange yet he was forced to think them out of his own experience. Had other souls found their way to this and the many other alien thoughts that David laboured with? And what is the connection between this process and the past, even the deep past, i.e., evolution? David needed this connection to be made for him for the sake of meaning. He knew that there is an intimate connection between perception and reality.

The very difficult thought that follows from this is that the world we habitually perceive today under ordinary circumstances, i.e., the world of "common sense", was created over time in a process beginning with perceptions that carried feelings of awe and wonder, just as David's did now. These perceptions were shared by a community of souls who together, affirmed its objective existence to one another. Works of art, literature, or simply speech were generated, expressive of this new emergent world. Finally, others who were not members of this original community accepted the concepts. Over time these concepts began to be perceived in the world, *as* the world and finally the world *became* this way and all perceived it to be so. As the world became this way, so too consciousness transformed, the structure required to perceive the world this new way. Tragically, in the course of this development, many other forms of consciousness were wiped out in genocidal madness of one kind or another.

David remembered poignant passages he had read in daVinci's Codex, i.e., the records of his scientific researches. He could feel the scientific mind just beginning to emerge and perceive the world in a new way, where it could be quantified and measured. At the same time, evidence of a mind still held in thrall by the majesty and wonder of *living* nature remained.

The difficulty for David lay in the appalling fact that nothing existed in current theories of evolution to support one shred of what he knew to be true. His search for meaning was in danger of being ship-wrecked and his doctoral program could evaporate in a cloud of idiosyncratic opinions.

The dominant theory of evolution, even with its many controversies around graduated or punctuated equilibrium was unassailably unified around one foundational "fact". Although David understood that although there was not a hope of verifying this "fact" with scientific methods, it remained as the core of any modern theory of evolution, since the time of Darwin.

The world, in all its diversity, selective mechanisms and so on, is readily perceived to be, as a matter of "common sense", factually solid—a collection of objects in space, separate from one another and perceivable with a clear perspective vision. Objects stand out in clear outline for us and our language expresses this fact in its prevalent use of nouns (*it is*, etc.). This world is correlative to an equally sharpened and acute sense of self that we enjoy today.

At the time that we were forming our modern theories of evolution, we also were reaching a pinnacle in our development of self-consciousness. So, we woke up to ourselves, our own separate existence as selves, precisely at the time that we woke up to the world that is correlative to that form of consciousness: a world of discrete sharply defined objects in space. We then developed theories of the origins of what we saw as if that had been the situation for all time! We simply assumed that how *we* saw the world was an independent fact, and projected that picture back into the remote past.

The solidity of the modern world with its principle of separateness is the underlying premise of all modern theories of evolution, even though it is completely unverifiable. We simply assume it through the principle of Uniformitarianism, an unproved principle that states that the present laws of nature have been the same for all time. This principle is the basis for carbon dating for example.

David's initiatory experiences had shown him the existence of other forms of consciousness and therefore, other real worlds, any of which under the right circumstances could materialize and become THE world for all of us. At the entry point of his doctoral program, several months before his all-important committee meeting, David was stymied. How could he hope to bring his discoveries into relationship with the available pool of ideas when from the outset, on theoretical grounds, his findings were to be excluded? He wanted to say that our modern solid world with its correlative modern self-consciousness was not ultimate in any way. It is *not* a universal objective fact for all time. We are *not* doomed to an everlasting non-participatory existence in which we are simultaneously aware of our separate lives in a world of solid objects forever without spiritual significance. We are *not* fated to a permanent condition of anxiety and the world is *not* fated to be exploited to extinction by our excesses.

All these dreadful outcomes are now simply a matter of choice.

David knew all this to be true but who else had found their way to the knowledge of this truth? He knew he had to find his community of souls in order to share the fruit of their efforts and with their help begin to shape the language necessary to make an attempt to assail the impregnable fortress of habit that encrusted modern thinking about our collective origin.

So it was in those early months of his program, as he was agonizing over the structure and content of his proposal to the committee, that three lines of poetry floated mysteriously into his consciousness:

> *The future enters us*
> *In order to transform itself*
> *Long before it happens*

And so Rilke entered David's life. He pasted those lines on a little notice board where he kept all the quotes that kept him going against waves of hopelessness. It was clear to David that Rilke had the requisite experiences of the same forming future that he had. Being a master poet, Rilke was able to express this new world in astonishing, accurate, and beautiful, living language. David drank it all in gratefully. He had found a fellow soul, from whom he could learn much. He met others as well and slowly began to distinguish among them. The pivotal difference for David lay in the distinction between those who *intuited* the existence of a new world that was emerging from within the modern alienated consciousness and could describe it in conceptual language or could render it in some art form like literature, and those who had actually *experienced* it through an initiation and could thus act as mouthpieces for its reality, expressing it in its own terms.

David needed both. The very structure of the new consciousness demanded it. On the one hand there is the need to objectify the spiritual contents *as* contents of ordinary modern consciousness and there is the need to express those contents in the way of a mouthpiece. A dual consciousness!

Rilke was clearly an initiate and mouthpiece: [81]

> *Press down hard on me, break in*
> *that I may know the weight of your hand,*
> *and you, the fullness of my cry.*

David needed also to meet souls of the first kind, those who could intuit and write conceptually about the qualities of the new world, its epistemology, ontology, and place in the evolution of consciousness. He found them all in England, all contemporary, and only one left alive at 99 years old (1997). They loosely called themselves the Inklings and comprised Charles Williams, C.S. Lewis, J.R.R. Tolkien, and most significantly of all, Owen Barfield.

Owen Barfield became David's spiritual mentor for the duration of his doctoral program. David became aware of capacities that they both shared. They each loved the imagination, understood its distinct reality, and felt its beauty. They each were conscious of imagination, a capacity that C.G. Jung called psychic consciousness which is a capacity to perceive, in actual experience, the images that form outer appearances.

---

[81]   (Rilke R. M., 1996, p. 127)

Owen Barfield was also a thinker, which David was not. He had spent his life articulating a single idea: the evolution of consciousness. The truth of the imagination was integral to this effort. Barfield knew that the only way to "get beyond" the distress of our modern consciousness lay in our acceptance of the imagination is a vehicle of truth, and in our ability to enter the inner world and learn how to perceive objectively. At present we understand such efforts as yielding only "subjective" results, telling us nothing about the state of the world around us. Barfield knew that we can indeed go "within" and discover the inner life of the world, objectively. And so he mentored David into the methodology, through the transmission of concepts that he, Barfield, had laboured to bring forth out of his own experiences.

One of these concepts was "historical imagination". Normally, as a matter of "common sense" the past, even the recent past is felt to be removed in a permanent way from today's consciousness. That is, we can remember the past but never again can experience the consciousness that belonged to that past. Childhood, for example, is a period in our lives that we may remember but the consciousness of a child is lost forever for the adult, even though it may be remembered nostalgically as a "lost paradisal connection with nature".

When Barfield was as young as twenty three, he demonstrated that past consciousnesses are indeed accessible to present consciousness and he wrote a book, *Poetic Diction* that showed how it can be done. But such knowledge only became available if we can give up some inveterate habits of thought. The most serious of these habits that Barfield spent a lifetime drawing to our attention belong to our modern structure of consciousness. Barfield called them *idol-space* and *idol-time.*

Barfield taught David how our consciousness is correlative to the world in which we live and that an evolution of consciousness means also an evolution of the world. They are distinct but can never be separated. If you like, consciousness is the inward aspect and the world of the senses is the outward aspect of reality. So, our modern consciousness perceives and conceives a world of separate objects in a space and time that appear completely independent of the observing consciousness. In fact they are correlative! Other consciousnesses of the past experienced space and time very differently to us, because they *were* different!

Barfield even went as far as to claim that the *intended* use of our modern consciousness is to re-enter the past through an act of will and to *become* that past consciousness. In this way we are voluntarily returning to that participation with the world that our ancestors enjoyed involuntarily. This act overcomes the anxiety provoking separation that we suffer so much today.

David was thrilled to have found such a mentor. He had all the prerequisite experiences to appreciate and understand what Barfield was transmitting to him. Barfield's conceptions entered David through osmosis. He began to speak the same language without effort and his program began to take shape. He had already begun to formulate some ideas of his own before he met Barfield. For example he knew intimately about entering, and being entered by, an image. His "animal image" experiences were quite conclusive on that score, but until now, outside of shamanism he had found no collaboration in scholarship. Furthermore, David's experiences were spontaneous. Barfield was able to take him much further by talking about entering the image (of the past) voluntarily, through an act of will.

David began to experiment with historical imagination, linking it theoretically with the field of phenomenology. This link in effect gave David his methodology for his doctoral research. His first attempt was simple. He was at one of his doctoral seminars, organized by the school he had enrolled in. As part of the introduction to this all-important seminar on methodology for doctoral candidates, the leader asked all the participants to remember the flight over. So David did:

> *I first get an image of a plane flying high. I must be outside the plane in order to see it this way. I see the clouds and the deep reds and pinks that line the upper surfaces. Now I am inside the plane. I can smell the air-conditioned staleness. A sound now catches my attention in the seminar room. It is the air-conditioning and I spontaneously associate that sound to the ever present steady thrumming of the airplane engines, just outside my window. Now a thought intervenes about whether I*

am following instructions. It passes as I see D. (a fellow learner who came across with me on the same flight) a few seats behind me down the narrow passage way of the plane. We are leaving Seattle, pulling away. The engines drone on. I begin to wonder if "pulling away" is the right metaphor for me. Does it evoke the memories of my departure from Seattle? I felt many things as I left Seattle to come here. As soon as the plane took off I fell asleep so tired. The night before I had a sleepless night, much conflict! I wondered if I would even make it to the seminar. My God! The tensions in life are so huge these days. Yet we are finite creatures. How much can we hold? Someone knocks on the door of the seminar room but I return to my conflicts. By the time I got to the airport, I was tired and depleted. I learned that the flight will be delayed so sit quietly there for a couple of hours until D. arrives. I can do that—sit quietly, that is. I had to learn how. I had had severe symptoms for many years which were very painful and could not be ameliorated. So I had to learn how to find a still place within myself even with the pain. So now it is easy for me to do.

So, now I sit and look out of the window to the tarmac where giant birds are taking off in the pouring rain. Looking closely I can see that just when the plane leans back to soar, conditions are just right to create a narrow band of water streaming back from the very tip of the wing. I am struck by the graceful slender curve it makes as it ribbons behind the wing. So many huge forces must come into play to create that stream, somehow coordinating into a whole at just the right moment to create a frail transient thing of beauty—just for a moment.

At this time of remembering during the seminar, David first experienced the memory as "in the past," i.e. something he did *then*. This separated David "now", from David "then" by a felt distance in time. The memory was available to him now but the consciousness held within the memory was not, thus the experience was not available to him now with that temporal "distance" in place.

Quite a few accounts read in the seminar had a similar feel to them so David did not feel an emergence of the *past-as-present* in the description as much as a report of something that had happened in the past. The vitality of lived immediacy was missing in the accounts.

For the past to have the quality of lived immediate experience, something must happen to collapse the separation between the co-researcher "now" and the co-researcher "then". David felt it happen several times when he entered the "past" and it became alive and immediate while in other places, he felt a distance grow between himself and the memory. The "life" in the memory then waned and his awareness drifted back into the seminar room.

When he did succeed in merging with his own memory, i.e., he experienced the scene once more with the *consciousness* of that recent past, a surprise occurred. He recovered an aspect of the experience that was not previously conscious. This surprise was particularly strong in the moment when he once again noticed the stream of water coming off the edge of the wing tip.

His act of reflection concerning the tremendous forces that must have combined to form this fragile thing of beauty was new. This showed David that the consciousness held in the memory had become available to him now, at the seminar. He had found a way to enter the memory with his present consciousness and make a hidden aspect of the experience available to him now. David had succeeded in interpenetrating with an image of the past, *as an image himself.* Thus, it no longer made sense to talk only of the stresses that combined together to form a thing of beauty at the wingtip of the airplane. Those stresses equally "belonged" to him and so offered the possibility of his creating a thing of beauty, like a stream of water arcing back like a rainbow from the tips of his wings.

David had succeeded through an act of will to enter a past form of consciousness, ever so briefly ending the state of alienation that is so crippling today for us all.

With this early success, David enthusiastically looked for other souls who, like Barfield were exploring the same domain. He found his way to Robert Graves and his analeptic method; C.G. Jung and his method of active imagination; D. H. Lawrence's "blood imagination"; and of course

Rilke. In David's view, this capacity to surrender yet remain conscious until the interiority of the *other* is felt as a living reality found its greatest practitioner in Rilke. His poetry is a record of such encounters with *other* by a consciousness able to be a vessel for the manifestation of the *other* into the human being. David loved the quote he found in the beginning of one of Rilke's books: [82]

> *In the elegies we find ourselves in a kind of visionary landscape*
> *where things are both familiar and unfamiliar, and where the*
> *distinction between inner and outer seems to have been abolished,*
> *or transcended.* [This] *can only be conveyed by means of words*
> *which, that they may achieve the necessary incantation, must be*
> *given, by means of rhythm, emphasis, and context, particular*
> *shades and depths of meaning.*

David slowly began to understand that such ideas were currency among a growing community of souls. His own experiences were not merely idiosyncratic. They were a melody in a swelling chorus of voices, each expressing the same theme. There *is* a way after all of overcoming our alienation from nature. Over hundreds of years we have succeeded in developing a sharpened sense of a self awareness coupled with a world that can be measured, quantified, and no longer expressive of meaning. We then developed theories, particularly theories of our origin that hardened this configuration into an unassailable habit of thought, i.e., the world is and *always was* the way a newly acquired self-aware consciousness had merely begun to perceive it. David found two other members of his community of souls that eloquently capture our predicament. T.S. Eliot writes: [83]

> *What are the roots that clutch, what branches grow*
> *Out of this stony rubbish? Son of man,*
> *You cannot say, or guess, for you know only*
> *A heap of broken images, where the sun beats*
> *And the dead tree gives no shelter, the cricket no relief,*
> *And the dry stone no sound of water . . .*

---

[82]   (Rilke M. R., 1939, p. 6)

[83]   T. S. Eliot: *The Waste Land*

More prosaically, from the field of philosophy, Richard Tarnas summarizes these urgent warnings in terms of our history of ideas: [84]

> *Thus the cosmological estrangement of modern consciousness initiated by Copernicus and the ontological estrangement initiated by Descartes were completed by the epistemological estrangement initiated by Kant: a threefold mutually enforced prison of modern alienation.*

David now knew that this deplorable existential condition was not always so and need not be so in the future. In fact a growing number of people were discovering for themselves that the consciousness of the past was not the same as it is now and that our present consciousness is itself transforming. There is nothing final about our modern state of mind and the world it inhabits.

David's excursion into his recent past, following Barfield's method of historical imagination, demonstrated two crucial facts. One is that we still do participate in the world through our unconscious and second, we can re-enter that state of participation through an act of will and discover a world once again expressive of meaning. David had after all discovered that the enormous stresses he perceived in the wing of the airplane which created a form of great beauty, were also expressive of a process also going on within him, along with its intuited outcome.

Others in David's new community of souls knew this participatory world too and were beginning to express it in artistic ways. Owen Barfield was for David a pre-eminent spokesman for the underlying theory that could begin to orient our Western culture towards this world, first intellectually then in actual experience. But David knew the obstacles were formidable. We do not give up hardened habits of thought that easily. Barfield himself likened the transformation in our modern culture to that of overthrowing the former "Aristotelian mindscape", a painful and bloody chapter in our history.

---

[84]   (Tarnas, 1991, p. 419)

Everything Barfield had to say was a balm for David and he soaked Barfield's thought into his own being. It no longer mattered to David where his own thoughts ended and Barfield's began. There was a soul connection between them that was alive and vital. Barfield gave David the words to bridge between scholarship and his inner experiences and David was deeply grateful to him. Knowing that Barfield also had endured a spiritual crisis in his own life when he fully felt the schism between ordinary life and his own inner riches, gave David added courage to continue.

The greatest gift Barfield gave David was an unintended one. On the 14th December, 1997, a date David would never forget, Owen Barfield died. The very day that David's doctoral program was accepted by his committee, his mentor died!

During the course of his long life, one that spanned the 20th century, Barfield had written and spoken on one theme and one theme only: the evolution of consciousness. David's own experiences had drafted him into service of this same theme. He felt the timing of Barfield's death as a synchronicity. He did not feel that he had to carry on Barfield's work in the way that Barfield did, that is, theoretically. David could not do that! But he did feel that Barfield had become an ancestral soul in his own life, still speaking to him, still conveying the concerns of the ancestors to him and the other members of his community of souls.

The ancestral concerns that both Barfield and David keenly felt were for the very survival of the world. Barfield had developed the concepts that could best serve those efforts to avert disaster, whereas David had the direct experience of an initiate who had personally gone through the kind of ordeal that opened him to the reality of what Barfield was taking about. David could best advance Barfield's own work by assisting other individuals who also were feeling the same forces of transformation within their own being. He knew the road signs and with Barfield's help could provide the necessary concepts to aid understanding, while accompanying the individual through the transforming experience.

John C. Woodcock

Mouthpiece

One of the most endearing qualities of being human is that once we are given a gift from the divine realms, we spend the next many years still searching for the gift in the world of senses when all the while we are in fact becoming that gift.

Master John: *Aphorisms*

David had at last discovered meaning in his life, uniting everything he had struggled with for so many years. He had, for years felt an irreconcilable split between the spiritual realms and the ordinary world of the senses. His "abandonment" by both realms led him to his *passion* in which he gained an ability to see clearly and objectively while still in the incarnate world of the passions. He also understood what being a mouthpiece implied: a reappraisal of the ordinary world of the senses, which he had so far undervalued. He had to embrace the ordinary world as it is, not as he might want it. He had to become as ordinary as possible, i.e., by simply accepting his own ordinariness. Only in this way could he possibly make the distinction in felt experience between his own ordinariness and the presence of the *other* within.

This is a true polarity! The more ordinary I am the more the extraordinary can incarnate in an ordinary life. The more I separate from the source the more the source can find itself in me!

Shortly after his commitment to ordinary life, David had a dream that seemed to support and deepen that stance:

> *I am alone, in a strange large city, perhaps to visit a friend . . . At some point I wander and get lost. I find my way into the city deep. In a bar, with strangers . . . I stand and watch. One man, possibly gay, gets me a stool. I go sit at a table and the scene becomes or merges with a vast amphitheatre. A swell of people are flooding into it: devotees of a master. He has come. The tide of people rushing by me and he is there. I prostrate myself at his feet.*
>
> *He and I seem to be alone. He touches me and the kundalini energy rises again to the top of my head. Bliss!*
>
> *Apparently my friend has found me a bed to sleep in. I wake up later and I say I need to write down my experience with the master. Someone casually remarks that he died last night. I am shocked as I begin to discern the meaning of our encounter.*

As I walk down the street, sure enough I begin to feel his presence within as if I am being lifted by the seat of pants. Get going, he says, laughing.

Now there is a scene where I am planning with others a group of Catholic churches, no boundaries, open.

My friend finally finds me but now everything had changed. My purpose is totally different. I now know all the years of preparation, of dual reality, of being penetrated by the other, *are a preparation for the master to arrive, to enter me.*

Years of preparation simply to receive the master! Dual reality, becoming the other, *he using my senses, so many years, simply to be ready for him.*

The master dies, no more looking outside for the master no more waiting: Get going!

Without becomes within.

Death and resurrection of the master!

And so, with some regret, David turned his attention away from the splendour of the inner realms (or maybe they turned from him) and towards that realm he had badly neglected and indeed the coin of that realm—money!

He felt as though he had recently been born. Everything seemed fresh and he was open to what the world would offer. He was certain that he had been drawn into service and was quite open to what the future might bring. At the same time he still laboured with the old belief that the future was in some way an extension of the past and so the first work he looked for lay in the field of counselling where he had worked for the past twenty years or so. He sought out institutions where, he believed, the money lay. He was desperate for some steady income.

His son was now 15 years old and they had both relocated to Sydney, Australia where David had lived for the first half of his life. Now, David was down to his last few hundred dollars and he had another problem.

When he sat down to write a resume, his record of "past employment" with names, dates and so on, was a disaster! Unfortunately for David, his previous employment had mostly been in private practice, scraping by week by week. He had shunned institutions for the most part and seeking work in agencies or universities, even with his Ph.D. in hand, therefore raised considerable difficulties for him.

It was time to be creative!

Luckily his "past employers" were all in the USA and he did have some evidence that he had worked in various places as a consultant from time to time. He did have an undergraduate degree in science, a master's degree in Educational Psychology and a doctorate in Consciousness Studies. He had also been licensed as a therapist. Perhaps he could stretch matters a little. David cobbled a packet together that he thought he could live with and also avoid the one interviewer's question that terrified him:

Where exactly have you been these last twenty years?

David's resume carried much more meaning for him than merely as a device to get him hired somewhere. He was stunned by the lack of continuity in his documented history. Whereas many other people could construct a narrative that at least seemed like a smooth thread from past to present and then towards the future (my plans etc.), David's resume looked like he had temporarily surfaced somewhere in the historical flow and then disappeared out of sight again for some years, again and again.

Where exactly have I been in those gaps of time?

The human ego seems to require the fiction of continuity in time so that it can be assured of its stable existence. Yet how flimsy this fiction is as an anchor in life! How easily undermined! Consider this for example: When we each emerge from sleep each and every day, there is a moment when we could ask: Who am I? We do not know who we are just for a moment and then memory comes in and fills the gap, assuring us that we are continuous with yesterday. We even assimilate our dreams to what happened yesterday so that yesterday becomes affirmed and the dream disaffirmed.

This being so, it is very frightening when the ego cannot make the link. We even have names for this kind of pathology: dissociative disorders or even a fugue state. In fact memory gaps are very common. We just don't like it.

Now we come to the question! What happens if you no longer need that anchor? What happens if you do not require anchoring yourself in that or any fiction at all?

Master John: *The State of Modern Psychology*

What David had been through for twenty years or so was real. He had no doubt about that! But what was the nature of that reality? It clearly was not and could not be understood in terms of common categories of experience. What *could* he call it? *Shamanic Studies, Kundalini Experience?* What about *Encounters with Yet Unknown Futures, Initiation into Future Consciousness.* All these were true yet naming them this way simply proved how far he had been marginalized. He wrote his thesis within the only recognized academic field that could address his experiences at all: Consciousness Studies with a first person methodology.

His commitment to "join the human race", to embrace his own ordinariness brought with it a felt obligation to somehow render his arcane experiences intelligible to others. He dreamed he was talking a language that no one understood. Yet he had to keep trying. How many times did he have to say, "No, I don't mean that"?

He had been reborn, an old personality was stripped away, dismembered, washed, loosened—there were many metaphors that his dreams showed of the process. And he had entered an *in between state* in which both time and space were qualitatively different from our usual mechanical sense.

He could describe his time sense not by a clock, but by the larger cycles of movement that informed his imagination. For example, there was that time in his journey marked by sequences of expansion and contraction—a most painful period. He would be filled with enthusiasm for a new project or a Centre, etc. and then contracting forces would hit him with doubts about money, whether it was what he was meant to do, whether he had deliberated long enough and so on. He learned that during this time transiting Saturn was conjunct his natal Jupiter and so these ancient images of qualitative time gave objectivity to his experience, i.e., he had been simply in that time and had to take account of it until it passed.

His spatial sense was also very different and could not be described in the usual sense of being characterized by solid objects separated by distance, along with perspective. The space that David lived in was qualitatively close, not empty, but rather wisdom-filled with objects interpenetrating one another.

This reality dominated most of David's being for over twenty years and his memory of it was excellent! Yet from the ordinary perspective he had simply disappeared from view, leaving no trace, no record of the passage of ordinary time. Questions such as, "What did you do on the weekend" were simply meaningless or even unintelligible to him. And if he tried to say what had occupied his time over the weekend, he was in turn rendered unintelligible.

David's unconscious fear of losing all connection with the ordinary world (even with his secret undervaluation of it) had manifested in an obsession with his *papers*. He paid what bills he could on time; he did his taxes carefully; made sure he had a current passport; and kept accurate records of his transactions in the community. He kept all transcripts of his academic achievements, licenses, and certificates of merit. Any mention of his name in print was carefully filed away. He had letters of reference dating back fifteen years.

In other words, out of his fear of being seen as an "illegal alien", he made doubly sure that no one could doubt his credentials or suspect that he was not qualified to do whatever job he was doing. He exerted tremendous effort to maintain the fiction that his outer life was continuous in time. He struggled to represent each moment of his life as being accounted for and logically related to the next. In fact David was living the impossibility of two kinds of memory, two contiguous yet apparently irreconcilable pasts. He did not have the faintest idea how to live this way.

Nonetheless he somehow had to.

Now armed with his largely fictitious resume, David applied for three different jobs in Sydney. The most attractive ones appealed to his history as a counsellor. He applied for the position of Clinic Director in a private organization and a School Counsellor at a private school. The least favoured application was for a position as a Mathematics teacher at the same private school. David had an undergraduate degree in maths some thirty years ago and really had no intention of working as a teacher in any school, let alone as a maths teacher.

As he was driving his car to the interview for the position of School Counsellor, he received a phone call letting him know that he had been a serious candidate for the position of Clinic Director BUT we are so sorry . . . This news alarmed him considerably and he redoubled his intention to land the School Counsellor job. He arrived at the interview highly focussed and single minded. When the Principal said they had chosen a local person for the Counsellor position but they needed a maths teacher to start right away, David simultaneously felt the floor slip away and a deeper knowledge that calmly said I will take the job that is offered. They were a little surprised that he did not go away to think about it but hired him on the spot to do a job that David had been certain he would not have to do, ever!

Our society is built on a kind of altruism which simply means working on behalf of others. Almost every job available today exercises this altruism. This is quite different from selfless service though in the sense that normally in our jobs our secret ambitions or desires are left quite unexamined and seem irrelevant to the enactment of the work. It does not matter if the auto mechanic is enraged at his boss, beats his wife, or is a drug addict, as long as he can perform his functions, serving others by fixing their cars.

This is not so with selfless service. One of the enduring qualities of selfless service is that she feels drafted into service, often against her will. The service is often in a form that comes as a huge unpleasant surprise. Yet, strangely, when the draftee finally comes around after much suffering, to an acceptance, then will and desire amazingly synchronize and she finds that she is in fact happy in a way that seemed previously inconceivable. She would not will herself to be anywhere other than where she was willed to be.

This kind of service demands a unity of will and desire, in order to be available to others, unencumbered by divisions within the self.

Master John: *Lecture Series on Service*

The first year was unmitigated hell, with anxiety attacks; the second year was unendurable, with exhaustion; the third year was an uphill climb, living day by day with no hope; the fourth year found isolated islands of passable toil; the fifth year began to see fresh signs of new life and even moments of a strange feeling that David tentatively and provisionally dared to call:

Happiness!

David had undergone what could only be called a transformation of his personality over a period of twenty years or more but he now came to understand that the problem of manifesting that transformation in the context of an ordinary lived life still remained. His old personality had not simply disappeared. After all, his personal history still remained in his memory. His old hurts, childhood weaknesses, uninformed prejudices, were still readily available, stimulated at any moment by his new school environment. He also had another set of memories that assured him that something deep within had changed, or better, had come to birth. This relatively newer set of memories carried thoughts, feelings, and insights that were completely at odds with those of his old personality.

David was at the centre of a huge conflict within his soul!

Everything about the school offended him! He felt injected into a 19th century educational system. His day was regimented from start to finish. He was required to do a job and what he thought or felt about anything was irrelevant. Only performance mattered! Conformity in behaviour and record keeping were the guiding principles of conduct. The greatest attention went to the most trivial administrative detail, while pedagogical issues were far removed from any staff meeting. No discussions were allowed in formal settings. Instead the staff was given the facts to live by. The executive branch was in strict control with a rigid hierarchy. Power relations were the order of the day and professional staff members were treated only as employees.

The students obligingly reflected the system with a barrage of dysfunctional behaviour and incorrigible unwillingness to learn. Where the Executive insisted on uniformity and conformity, students scorned authority and questioned everything. The pedagogy of the school encouraged teachers to give the boys as many hand-outs as possible because "they accept pieces of paper and will write". Teaching, if that meant talking to the students was impossible because, from the boys' point of view, the teacher's voice was merely one more noise in the classroom din. If conversation meant an exchange between persons, then that art had disappeared with the dinosaur.

How many times had David been asked a question, considered his response, only to find the verbal momentum had immediately swept in an entirely new direction, leaving him speechless?

These working conditions caused an eruption in David's old personality. His prejudices against institutions or bureaucracies spilled out through an acute anxiety that exploded. The creaking floor board of this collapsing house of cards was a pervasive feeling of:

I can't cope!

At the same time, David had a core feeling that he had been placed here, in the chaos of a modern secondary school, where Generation *Y* was having nothing to do with the Baby Boomers who were their elders. The circumstances of his getting hired were compelling on this score and he did not ignore synchronicities. He knew that he had been relieved of money worries, while at the same time he had been given a job that forced him to strengthen those soul capacities he had developed, in circumstances that on the surface seemed uniquely designed to destroy those very capacities. The school, like most schools, functioned to destroy individuality!

As he did so often before, when faced with crippling isolation because of his unusual perceptions, David sought confirmation and consolation through literary companions. He found his way to John Gatto, a New York teacher who researched the *actual* goals of modern education as publically stated by the officials and educational leaders who had founded public education in the early 20th century—goals that are carried forward today in a routine manner by public education. Gatto quotes Alexander Inglis' 1918 book,

Principles of Secondary Education, in which six functions of schooling were spelled out: [85]

- "Adjustive" which establishes fixed habits of reaction to authority;
- "Diagnostic" which determines each student's "proper" social role;
- "Sorting" which trains individuals only so far as their likely destination in the social machine;
- "Conformitive" in which kids are to be made alike so future behaviour will be predictable, in service to market and political research;
- "Hygienic" which is polite code for tagging the unfit so clearly they drop from the reproduction sweepstakes;
- "Propaedeutic" in which a small fraction of kids will slowly be trained to take over management of the system.

David's old personality devoured this succinct and penetrating verification of what he also knew and felt. He felt armed in sea of hostility, ready to fire at any faint challenge to his certainty about teaching, love, children, individuality, and creativity.

No one could care less! The school was centrally concerned with one thing: the time table and how well David filled his allotted spaces. Complaints from parents were bad and immediate reparative action was required; complaints from teachers were ignored at best or treated with contempt; chaotic classrooms were dealt with by instruction on classroom management skills, no matter how seasoned the teacher. David was coached about what to say to parents on parent-teacher nights, and more importantly, what to avoid saying. At no time was he to refer to a "systemic problem" in the school. Each "behaviour problem" was to be discussed in isolation, as if the offending student were functioning in a vacuum.

To drive the issue of David's new status of "employee" home, the name tag he had to display on the table was invariably printed as "Mr.", never "Dr." as one might initially believe an educational institution would

---

[85]   (Gatto, 2012)

favour. David's thoughts or feelings were not required. His adequate performance as reflected in the yearly student averages *was* required. In fact there was one time that practice worked in his favour. An angry parent accused him of being a terrible teacher, not knowing how to do his job and had complained to the Curriculum Director who simply looked up the statistics and showed her that David's classes were, on average, the same as everyone else's.

The issue for the school was simply whether he, David, was functioning statistically as an outlier, or as data lying within one or two standard deviations of the mean. It did not matter the least what the parent or David was actually going on about, in regards to her son.

David was expected to inculcate a form of discipline based proudly and solidly on principles of behaviour modification, designed to shape student behaviour along the lines that Inglis had written so eloquently about, a century earlier. Where David wished to be empathetic, he was learning to be directive and uncompromising. He had to make snap decisions concerning justice (which boy was to be punished), and he had to learn how to stop students from arguing back at him. He broke up fights, issued detentions like lollies, told boys to shut up, get out, sit down, stand up, do the work, put your pens down, start writing, stop talking, watch here, heads down, listen, we'll be back at lunchtime, five, four, three, two, one . . . and "the next boy that does . . . I will . . ."

Professional advice form more senior colleagues at the school lay along the lines of, "Buddy, it doesn't matter who gets punished, as long as *someone* gets punished!"

Aah! David pondered,

I have finally met a spiritual adept who is working on behalf of impersonal cosmic justice!

Through this strange and unremitting torment of his soul, newly born and intending to enter the world with love and perhaps with some new perspectives on our collective future, David's old personality simply wailed,

Why?!!

And he was answered.

And he was answered from within, as always, with dreams:

> *I am at school. The senior deputy head and others accuse me of being phoney, of living a life that is false. Everyone who knew me had got together and shared what they knew. It appears that I "fit in" with the circumstances but who am I? If I am revealed, not in a role but as myself, I am rejected. Where will I go, what will I do? I plead for a job, I need to survive somehow. They are unmoved. The deputy simply brought me out to be myself, not in any role, but something more within the institution.*

> *I am in a school . . . It is time to teach a new class. Everyone is bustling around. I have nothing prepared at all . . . a new class of twenty students . . . my head of department asks me if my previous concerns have been addressed. I can't even remember what they were. I need to hand papers out but have none copied. I go to the class. They are waiting expectantly. I cannot find any white board marker to use. All through this, I am not anxious, simply moving on to the next step even though I must start and I have not done any of the usual preparations.*

> *It is as if I slowly become aware that indeed my time of teaching has arrived and everyone is ready, except for me, it seems. I become aware of it and just go with it.*

> *I am in a horse race in complete harmony with my horse. We are losing interest in the race but I keep speaking to him, praising him. We veer off to the right and now are out of the race. I become anxious. What will I do next? A voice comes:*

> *YOU MUST TEACH!*

David knew, i.e., from his new personality that perceived things very differently from his old one, that he was undergoing some kind of preparatory experience. He was meeting the world *as it is*, not as he might want it to be, or imagine it to be. He *could* function through his old personality, the one that he tried to capture on his resume, but as his dream said, he felt phoney doing so. His resume could make no mention of his new personality at all and nowhere in the school was he being encouraged to speak from his new personality. When he did, generally it went badly. People did not want to hear what he had to say. So, he quietened that voice and instead felt phoney.

Many years ago he had had a dream that seemed now to foreshadow his current predicament:

> *I am in India as an advisor to Gandhi. We are in Benares, the Holy City. He doesn't know what to do. I didn't know either but I acted on an intuition: "What do you do at any time in Benares?" He smiles and nods. He now knows what to do.*

> *Later on, I am asked to leave, take my things, go. As we leave the house, the others scatter and I am alone in a foreign city . . . feeling of being utterly isolated . . . no longer advisor to Gandhi who has his own destiny . . . no longer associated with the Man of Destiny, alienated, in a foreign country . . . separated from the one who is to become the GREAT SOUL, Mahatma. I experience great alienation . . . I need to attend to my personal effects. The Man of Destiny goes off to do great things. I remain behind, alone, isolated, not much of a personal life left. But I do now have one, in contrast to being his advisor where I had none.*

At that time his ordinary personality had been appropriated to the sacred task of assisting the greater personality to come into being. This task had been most demanding, having the effect of draining his resources and leaving his personal life in tatters. Everything had to be thrown into the task and he had been consumed by it.

David then had been released, task accomplished. He felt the enduring presence of an *other* within him. David came to call this mysterious *other* his new personality which seemed to exist simultaneously with his old familiar personality, both sharing his sensory nervous system. He had two sets of thoughts and perceptions!

He then had to return to ordinary life and regain a foothold. And money was the key resource for him. His job at the school was such a foothold. Even his old personality understood that. But he simply did not know *how* to do it. His dream with the deputy headmaster, and others like it, was clearly saying that he was to "continue in his work", not split with a feeling of phoniness, but with both personalities in play. And to make matters worse, all this had something to do with becoming a *teacher*!

It seemed to David there were two stages in the manifestation process that he was undergoing. The first involved a manifestation into the soul of a process that took over twenty years, and the second involved expressing that new reality in the context of an ordinary lived life. In this sense, one could say that the new personality has entered and is beginning to participate in the material world.

In this second process, David was, as it were, about five years old.

As much as his circumstances grated on him, so much so that his skin flared up and he had long bouts of a terrible fiery itching, David could not cleave to only one point of view. For example he hated most of what the deputy headmaster was doing, heard horrendous stories of his callousness towards staff, etc. Yet David had to acknowledge that the deputy headmaster's being that way was somehow instrumental to his own spiritual task of manifestation. David therefore could not align himself with any polarized position within the power dynamics of the school, as tempting and satisfying as it would be to do so.

David's deeper knowing understood that he was meeting the world as it is today. The school was a microcosm of the larger world. Everything that happened there happened anywhere. The power principle reigned supreme and love played no part in decision making.

Within this chaotic alchemy, David had received a dream mandate from within:

> *When you get out of the horse race you must become a teacher.*

> *Surely the dream does not mean I must become a maths teacher,*
> *that I am doomed to stay in this accursed school? What kind of*
> *teacher am I to become?*

The dream said nothing about what form of teaching David was to become. It was his old personality that asked that question. The dream simply said: "You must become a teacher once you are out of the horse race". David at least understood part of the dream language. In fact he had felt less and less inclined to "stay in the race". His ambitions and goal centred activities were drying up fast. He gave up searching for new jobs and instead focussed more carefully on the dream mandate.

His old personality became obsessed with the question of *form*, while his new personality simply generated an intention: to become a teacher, without knowing what form would be involved at all. From his old personality, David felt he had to do something to become a teacher. The problem was that he could only bring past experience to bear. He had already formed ideas of what a teacher was, or could possibly be, and on that basis found his work at the school totally and painfully incompatible. To make matters more stressful, he had a series of dreams which showed him totally unprepared to teach and yet the expectation was clearly for him *to teach*. And *now*! His old personality was greatly stressed by this mandate but his new personality took it in stride. It seemed as if on the one hand David clung to the past, to what he already knew while on the other hand he was quite comfortable orienting himself to the unknown future, ready to step into what has yet to come.

Dreams were showing him in relationship to great teachers, or masters. In one:

> *Lying with my wife, I enter the "in between place" consciously.*
> *I observe myself with the Dalai Lama. He is on his throne and*
> *I am on a chair, looking into each other's eyes. I look deeply into*
> *his great dark wells. There is nobody there, no form. Momentary*
> *terror! I feel compassion pouring out of that place of emptiness. I*
> *am given a mantra: compassion flows through emptiness.*

This did not make life easier for David:

Here I am, obsessed with the question of form and I am given an experience of "no form", emptiness and shown that compassion, love itself, flows through that condition.

David was beginning to feel that he did not know much about what to do after all. To help him along with that feeling another dream occurred, one in a rather long series, to do with humility:

I am in a room with Chuck Norris. He decides to meet me in combat after a playful spar in which I block one or two strikes. I now need to prepare for the fight. As I do so, we are moving towards a secret monastery outside town. I wonder increasingly what it is I think I am doing. There is no way in the world I can fight Norris. People are gathering in the auditorium. I try to practice by doing basic katas from my own training years ago—woefully inadequate. Who am I kidding? They will see through me completely. What a sham! This is a mockery. I move towards a young boy.

Now I am in a room. My bravado is useless. Any thought of "I know what to do" next slips away fast. In this room I am in the centre and others line the walls, watching. A young man comes up to me and shows me a book—a red box with a red string running through it. This is his solution to the problem of cause and effect.

"How long do you think I have been working on this problem?" he says, faintly mocking, "a good deal longer than you!" I do not have the faintest idea of what he is showing me. I feel humiliated, knowing nothing or near to it. The room erupts in chanting. More people go around the room, taking turns to chat about this or that existential problem. One man looking at me has tears of compassion for my plight.

I am being submitted to a barrage of knowledge that I know nothing about. It is an ordeal. I do not know what to do next and I begin to weep. All my own ideas, plans, purpose, are washed away in my ordeal.

The master is in the room too. I am left with no words. He gets up and moves away and I simply follow him. We enter ordinary reality, a house. He sits down and I come in. He says gently that I must not sit down, as we put on sandals. We are going to meet a great master who lives in ordinary life.

This dream and others like it produced a great relativisation of David's old personality. Up to this point, David had intuited that a question of form had emerged: what form should the "teacher" take in the world? He then almost immediately appropriated that question to himself and thought that he must come up with a form. Of course, he could only appeal to past forms through his memory and nothing worked. None of these past forms could adequately express the "new wine", the transformation he had undergone. It was very frustrating.

He was shown in no uncertain terms that even what he *thought* he knew was woefully inadequate to the task at hand. The author of whatever knowledge he had lay outside the ego, and thus was not subject to the will of the ego.

David's old personality was shown its rightful place through the agency of humility. He was learning to serve the master.

My wife and I are in India, a dry dusty street of a village. I see a wise man in the street talking loudly with great command in his voice. At first I look side on towards him but it becomes obvious he is directing his voice at me. He points to his feet where the mat is. I am to come to him, now! I do so and there is an old dusty prayer mat at his feet. Without much ado I simply get on my knees before him and prostrate myself. He continues to project his voice with great power in Hindi, over me. It sounds like an imperative of some sort. I go to kiss his foot but he shuffles it away—no that is not what is going on here i.e. supplication to the master. Rather it seems I am to be right there while he continues over me.

His voice is commanding and powerful. He is filled with a presence and uttering it. Like John the Baptist!

Then he disappears and I am left there with villagers gathering around and my wife nearby.

As David's failures to get out of the school into "something else that was more to do with my calling", mounted, he first grew angry, then discouraged, then fatalistic and finally, he surrendered. His new personality had felt all along that he had been *placed* at the school and was quite accepting of his "fate". He also could not ignore the compelling fact that his monetary worries were over. He was out of debt for the first time in his life and he and his wife had even invested in a property. He was able to support his son's efforts to get going in his own life and could afford to buy books whenever he wanted them and, with great pleasure, he bought tools to make repairs around the house. He never had wanted a new car but bought an old Ford for a few thousand so he and his son could drive around the city quite freely.

A very old and persistent anxiety began to loosen up in David and he began to trust in a way that had not seemed previously possible.

At school, his prejudicial stance towards the executive branch began to soften. Even with the daily replenishment of ammunition provided by incoherent decisions and contradictory explanations offered to the staff, David grew tired of arming himself and firing off a barrage of counter-attacks in the car on the way to work or as he returned home. He was wasting his energy in a battle he no longer wished to fight. The polarisation between just about every subgroup and its opposite was no longer of interest to David. Student behaviour was no longer a source of justification of David's own pedagogy or a means by which he could pillory the institution.

When other staff sought David's alliance against this or that "enemy" he did what he could not to alienate himself from his colleague and then withdrew to his little corner in the staff room to sit alone and . . . well, what WAS the next thing to do if those old ways were no longer viable, if fighting political wars, even in fantasy, were in effect to spin his wheels idly?

What does *it mean to serve the master?*

David ruminated.

The question of form, i.e., what form the teaching was to take, still approached him for attention and by now he understood that simply appropriating the matter to his ego and attempting to come up with a solution based on the past was folly. His dreams had worked their compensatory message on him to full effect.

In fact David remembered he had encountered this problem of form and ego before, while he was undergoing his transformation. The problem was linked to the mystery of karma.

Many years ago David had received a dream in which it was stated, quite simply: *You are a Knight Templar.* This dream led David to a study of the Knights Templar, their mission and their religious practices. A network of associations gathered around this study, and in his mounting excitement, David stumbled across their central vow of poverty, chastity, and obedience.

This vow was an image of a complex of thoughts, feelings, and actions that had plagued David most of his adult life. He always had ended up poor, without money, no matter what he tried. He undervalued the significance of sex in his own life, even though he was sexually active. And he tried to obey every dream image, or every piece of guidance from someone he considered wiser than himself. His slavish adherence to advice often led him into contradictory behaviour and he often failed to perceive ulterior motives in the advice which led to feelings of betrayal by the "elder". At times he felt cursed by this complex.

The dream carried a feeling of a memory, as if he were being reminded of a fact of a past life and so David began to explore the dream as an image of his karma. He hypothesised karma as the intrusion into modern life of an image of the past, acted out unconsciously by the one "bound by the past". His karmic link with the Knights Templar led him to strive to live his/their vow of poverty, chastity, and obedience literally. Yet he was in a modern context and the vow, so beautifully attuned to the conditions of the 12ᵗʰ century, was now obsolete and only produced a feeling of being out of tune with his own time.

David's question sharpened to:

How can I live my vow of poverty, chastity, and obedience in a modern context?

He recalled a time in his own life, even further back than his time of transformation. He had been only twenty years old, an undergraduate student and, like all students, in need of money. He got jobs as a truck driver for a biscuit factory and a drink company. In the morning he would get the delivery orders from his boss and for the rest of the day he was on his own, delivering the food and drink to the customers.

He loved the work! But why did he *love* the work?

Years later as he examined this historical fact as *memory*, it became clear to David that he loved working this way because an archetypal image was working through him in the context of an ordinary lived life:

In the morning he would receive instructions from the Father and then in complete freedom he carried out the Father's Will. His task was to dispense the loaves and the wine to the people. And this dispensation is an act of love!

Once David received the dream of the Knights Templar, and found his way to their vow of poverty, chastity, and obedience, he knew he had the image that could free him from his karma. To live this vow in the context of his ordinary lived life required first of all an exploration of the images embedded in the words themselves.

Poverty is a state of owning nothing. In what way could that be true today in a time when private property was felt to be almost a birth right? David's experiences with the deep psyche taught him that his feelings and the will, even his thoughts, do not originate in the ego. Emotions were like dreams, swelling wave-like into consciousness and then receding, leaving the ego to wonder, "What was *that* all about?"

What did the ego *own*? Even memory images changed over time. These considerations left David suddenly feeling impoverished! How did Plato and perhaps the Knights Templar know that poverty itself, the archetypal condition of poverty (Penia), is the mother of Eros, the god of love? This myth implies that we do not find love by trying to cure ourselves of neediness or feelings of impoverishment. On the contrary, only by entering such feelings is there the possibility of finding our way to love.

David began to understand the reality of his own condition of impoverishment. He owned *nothing!* And this feeling was the basis for entering the equally real conditions of chastity and obedience, as virtues supporting love in the world.

David was understandably disturbed to find an image of cutting at the bottom of the word chastity, as in castration. His researches took him to the priests of Cybele the Great Goddess, who voluntarily castrated themselves with her weapon of choice, the sickle, made in the shape of the new moon. He knew of monastic orders that denied the flesh for a higher purpose, i.e., celibates. He also had studied poets of love such as Rumi and Rilke who did not deny sexuality as much as unite sexuality with the highest spiritual aspirations. His own kundalini experiences opened him up to the sexual practices of shamans with their techniques of ecstasy and mystics who engaged in sexual practices designed to subordinate "lower desires" to higher aims. This often led to a brutal regime of denial, renunciation, and self mortification. But such practices also lead to an intensification of sexual passion which becomes an engine for transformation. In this sense castration means a voluntary sacrifice of outer expression for the sake of inner attainment.

The "cutting off" was only a preliminary step, to open the way to inner being no longer entangled with the demands of desire aimed at the furtherance of unconscious life.

A birth takes place in the chaste human heart, a virgin birth, and a love is born that is pure in the sense that desire is purified of its attachments in the outer world—a condition of poverty and chastity—emptiness, out of which flows compassion.

David now could feel the reality of his vow of poverty and chastity because he could certainly feel the stirrings of a love within his soul that was clearly *other* in its nature, leaving him feeling "in poverty", i.e., he could not possess it or claim it as his own. Furthermore it was a love that did not commingle with his personal desires at all. Rather it seemed to desire him, David. He felt himself to be the object of a divine desire, which was its own source, thus virginal in quality, or chaste.

David had found a way to make the vows of poverty and chastity real in the context of his life now, today. He did not have to act them out literally in any way, nor did he have to renounce them as obsolete. Those vows of the past which "plagued" him in the present through unconscious patterns of behaviour were transformed from historical fact into *conscious* soul realities, every bit as real to him now as they were then to the Knights Templar. David was now conscious of their operations within his soul life. He could for example practice the art of "not owning anything" by noticing the waves of emotions that sweep through us from time to time, or by paying close attention to unbidden thoughts or images that arise, without having to claim them as his, or not his for that matter. When desires arose in him, either attraction or repulsion, he could now experience them without "owning" them or even assigning a direction to them, such as "I desire that out there." Rather he was the recipient as much as the author of the desire which was a signal that love was present.

Now, fifteen years later, working reluctantly as a maths teacher in a secondary school in Sydney, David was to learn the meaning of the last part of the vow of the Knights Templar—*obedience* or, as he put it, *service to the master*.

We so often hear today the spiritual imperative to be immediate, to be here and now, and to be present to what is. There is of course profound wisdom at bottom here, wisdom that points us to the REAL. To be fully present is to perceive Absolute Reality.

This must be a rare and exceedingly difficult permanent attainment. Think about it! Many people indeed get glimpses of Reality, and it has the phenomenology of an epiphany, or at least great insight into the nature of things. For a moment, we are the happy recipients of an image of the Real, an image not determined by the past. Then what do we do? We seem to have the incorrigible habit of taking that image, once conscious, and holding onto it, making it into an ideology, a belief system, even an identity, using it to advance the aims of our egos.

Meanwhile the spirit moves on, ever ready to continue its forming activities, while we satisfy ourselves with the already formed, thinking we are still close to spirit.

I suspect that the idea of permanent attainment is an illusion. Rather, I think that, while we are in our "separateness", we must develop those capacities that prepare us for an encounter with the Real. Then we work to understand what happened. In that way we can bring the fruit of the encounter into the context of our ordinary and separate lives.

We might even say that this is the way of manifestation *of the Real into ordinary lived life.*

Master John: *Commentaries*

David felt a surge of anger rise up, empowering his voice.

It would be easy to react right now. This kid has pushed me far enough. Here I am trying to teach this new section and he simply won't shut up. Worse, he is sitting with his back to me, ignoring even basic courtesy. Some kids will look towards the front even as their eyes glaze over but he won't even pretend.

I could let it rip right now. The power of my shout would jerk his body around alright and I would get some vindictive pleasure from that.

But David had seen too much of that approach. His school was based on the pedagogical principle of power over others and shouting, even screaming, at a class room full of boys was the educational tactic of choice. He had on occasion, during a free period, wandered along the halls of the school listening to the angry shouts of the teachers, or the derisive hoots of the students. It did indeed feel like he was a zoo keeper of some sort, keeping the animals at bay. The deputy headmaster was well aware of the problem. Every day at noon he would enter each room via the speaker system and shout over the teacher and students, effectively modelling the very behaviour that he sought to stamp out in others. From his office, he could easily hear the hoots and whistles and screams and would, of course, threaten and cajole everyone into compliance, so that he could get his own important messages across, such as how tired he is of seeing all the garbage dropped in the schoolyard. Some animals, it appeared to David, were bigger than others and made bigger noises that trumped the moment.

David had tried this tactic early on in his job at the school and quickly learned that it was a simple reward-punishment system.

Students quickly learned that there was no reason to stop their behaviour until the teacher was reduced to a barrage of verbal abuse. Their rudeness was amply rewarded by the spectacle of a red faced spitting adult whose eyes were almost popping out of his head. They knew equally well that, no matter what, the teacher cannot physically touch them. These students were not fools. They were acutely aware of their legal rights at school and if they wanted to see a grown adult put on a great show of a frenzied berserker, all they had to do was talk over him for fifteen minutes or so.

Then it would be on and they would be provided with some great talking points during recess.

David had also participated in an incident which forever closed the door on this option for him. He was in a year seven class—the youngest boys of the school were here. These boys were not inured to verbal violence yet. And various teachers used this vulnerability to good effect when they wanted to assert their dominance over the boys.

One day David was attempting to teach a point when a boy down the back was failing to pay attention and so David punched out a command:

Look this way!

Sure enough, the tardy boy jerked up and looked this way but David simultaneously noticed something else. Perhaps his new personality "saw" it with the inner eye. The soul of another boy near the front quivered, as if struck violently with a club. His body registered the quiver like the surface effect of a subterranean earthquake and his eyes sprung wide open.

David was in turn shocked. And he got it. Never again would he adopt this practice. Instead, he would develop a repertoire of responses that would render such a blunt device unnecessary.

He would never do such a disservice to the soul again. The magnitude of the traumatized souls at school and by implication in the modern world staggered David. People were reduced to robotic imitation of themselves in the name of what! Compliance! It was nauseating and yet here he was working, no, *living* in such a system.

A year later, he was again confronted by a disruption to the class which made it impossible to go on with the lesson.

How can I respond in a new way, if I refuse the big stick approach?

Right now there was something missing in the room. David felt its absence in himself. There was clearly a power struggle going on. That feeling was seeping into every corner. The boys were watching carefully beneath their casual "couldn't care less about you" demeanours. David was poised with his white board pen suspended in the air as if waiting for an inspiration which would lead it once again to its sole purpose in life, to empty itself onto the board in scribbles that meant nothing to the boys. His body was half turned from the board to the offending rebel so that he looked like he had been arrested in the moment of a delicate step of a graceful, complicated dance.

The anger swirled in him, seeking an outlet, any outlet. Throwing something at the boy would be deliciously satisfying. Maybe storming down the aisle and snatching his diary with the inevitable "you are now on detention" would bring instant relief too. Some timely well-aimed sarcasm would not only stab the boy in the heart but would bring the added benefit of bringing the other boys on side temporarily in a horrible conspiracy of derisive scapegoating.

Something is missing here!

David's old personality was being rocked by the force of the rage that threatened to obliterate all discrimination. At the same time his new personality was untouched by the violence of the storm that raged within. David was simultaneously a leaf in the whirlwind and the eye of the storm.

The eye began to see!

David noticed the boy's posture which was slumped as if lacking in vital energy. While his face was set in a grimace that said I will take what you give and pay you back double, his hands and arms were limp as if the boy had no fight in him at all. David remembered that this particular boy had been to four schools previously, being expelled each time for angry non-compliance. He also was child of a bitter and acrimonious divorce currently ongoing.

Then David arrived at a moment of what can only be called *objective cognition*.

Our scientific revolution gave us each the capacity to be relatively objective about objects in the external world. This kind of objectivity is won at the expense of our desires and passions which are systematically excluded from such observations. They are not felt to reveal scientific knowledge. But scientific objectivity is notoriously vulnerable to incursions from our emotions or desires as is well known in the legal system with its research into the reliability of witnesses, and indeed within science itself, with its constant rejoinder to remain dispassionate. To attain scientific objectivity the observer must in some sense leave his body of desires, passions, and indeed images, and rise to a calm place where he can see . . . what? The vision gained by such objectivity is easily recognizable—a world of objects, no longer expressive of spiritual reality, simply a collection of dead objects in space that can be quantified and manipulated. This is the world we live in today and its inner correlative is scientific, i.e., "out of the body" objectivity.

But objective cognition is another matter altogether. Put simply it could be called an awakening to a new world from *within* the life of the body with its desires, impulses, and passions. This new world is perceived by a new personality that is born from within the old personality. This new world arises from within and transforms the present world so well described by science and now lived by us all.

David had learned of this new capacity within himself during his own time of transformation. He had a number of dreams that had a huge impact on his understanding of the problem of desire. One such dream showed him that his desires were in fact *the way* to a deeper perception of reality—a perception of reality born from within desire unfulfilled. Or perhaps the very fulfilment of desire lay in the perception itself:

> *Underground in a tunnel, a subway . . . a small cart comes along the tracks with gifts, one for me, with my name on it. A juggernaut, a subway train, comes and pushes the cart back into the tunnel where I can't reach it. I follow it, to get my parcel and I arrive at a terminal and am shown the wrappings of the gifts by a man. The gift is gone. I feel bereft, isolated.*

Then a scene opens up on the world stage. Gorbachev and Yeltsin
are working on a plan. Yeltsin says: Well let's come back later
and do some more. Gorbachev looks at him very tenderly and
embraces him with real warmth, between two former advisors.

In the dream, David's personal desire was thwarted and yet he followed
it "into the tunnel". From within that frustrated desire a perception of a
process going on "in" the world arose. The fact that Gorbachev is "Piscean"
and Yeltsin "Aquarian" deepens the mystery to one of a transition of
ages. David's own desires were the initiatory vehicle of deeper objective
perceptions of reality that lay within and beyond the desire realm itself.
They were *objective* cognitions because they emerged from a source that
itself was beyond desire, and thus not informed by desire. Yet, strangely,
one required the desire realm to get there. They were not separate and
the visions one attains are quite different from the fruits of scientific
objectivity. These objective cognitions are in effect an experience of a new
world, one in which objects regained their status as expressions of spiritual
realities. For example, David had received a glimpse of the spiritual reality
within the (then) recent political turmoil in Russia.

These inner experiences sensitized David to resonant examples in the world
and he found a particularly compelling image of the same process in the
Mel Gibson's movie: *The Passion of Christ*. For about twenty minutes or
so, Jesus is subject to torments that would take any man into the madness
of pain. Within that Passion, the Christ speaks and keeps speaking with
a wisdom that seems quite untouched by the whirlpool of suffering that
assails the man Jesus. It seemed to spring from the eye of the storm. He
says simply:

Father, forgive them. They know not what they are doing.

It seemed to David that the Passion of Christ was perhaps an initiatory
vehicle carried out literally on the body of Jesus, leading to the final
sacrifice on Golgotha. The "intent" of this mystery, as much as humans
can discern spiritual intentions, is to create what was not on earth before:
the human capacity for objective cognition, a capacity to perceive and
therefore draw forth a new world out of an old one. The "old world" is
the world that was painstakingly formed by a relentless process of taking

the spirit out of nature, removing our participation in nature as spiritual beings, and leaving us with an acute self-consciousness and a crippling state of collective anxiety from the paralysing condition of our isolation from nature and divinity. Science is the instrument of such a process.

The "new world" that objective cognition brings is one in which the world renews its status as expression of spiritual reality and our own status as participants in that reality is resumed voluntarily with an act of will.

Jesus was a Great Initiate, whose supreme sacrifice brought a new capacity to birth in human beings and thus made it available to others who also must undergo a similar initiatory process, although not literally so, as that work has been accomplished and does not need to be repeated.

David's own experiences were transformational and did bring to birth in him this new capacity of objective cognition. He also had been abandoned by both the community and the divine and so "went to the cross" where he remained for some time until the new capacity was born in him. Then, unlike the Great Initiate who came before him, David had to climb down from his cross and resume ordinary life. His was a most reluctant repatriation.

Back in the classroom, a *kairos* opened up for David. [86] He saw and acted in one breath, in perfect freedom. He perceived the boy as a crumpled piece of paper. There was no fight left in the boy. His aggression was a desperate bravado to stave off despair. His body could sustain his hostility no more and all he wanted was to be left alone by abusive adults. He would however fight to the death to prevent his frailty from being seen. After all he had to, simply had to survive somehow. He was near his limit.

David acted:

Just go on with your work boys!

---

[86] *Kairos* is Greek word pointing to a pregnant time, or an opportune time for right action.

The anger in David had disappeared and something else had entered, something that was decidedly missing in the room before. He felt its presence in his heart where before his heart had swollen with a feeling he had named as anger. Yes it is possible to have a wrathful heart but there must be more to it. What was that old saying from the Old Testament that David had remembered without knowing why? O Yes:

> *I have been looking for someone among them to build a wall and man the breach in front of me, to defend the country and prevent me from destroying it . . .*

In holding that wrath in his heart, David had brought forth from within that wrath itself a new quality that he could only call love. A transformation had occurred in his heart. It had arisen along with his objective cognition. His was a perception of the boy based in love. And it led to an action that eluded all expectations of the boys.

An increment of love had entered the world where there was none before.

Outwardly everything went on as before. David did write an email to the boy's pastoral counsellor asking him to remind the boy that basic courtesy is required in class and that "we would prefer to keep him at school, rather than have him expelled yet again." The usual class disturbances continued. Rudeness and obvious disinterest in the subject prevailed. However, some small signs that something had changed began to appear.

After class one day some weeks after this event, one boy approached David and asked, "Sir, how come you never get angry at us?" David did in fact get angry many times but the boy was pointing to something in the way he was experiencing David's presence in the class room. David didn't believe the boy was seeking an interpretive answer as much as an acknowledgement of his sense of things being different in David's classes. More boys were beginning to make similar kinds of observations. They were groping towards understanding something that they were feeling in their bodies. They watched David like hawks, as he responded to each new conflict that erupted.

On one occasion, a fight broke out in class with the usual ensuing chaos of boys egging it on or trying to break it up. They were astonished to see that David made no attempt to stop the fight. They would have understood if he had roared at them to stop or strode in using his own force to arrest the boys and send them to the office. All that was familiar territory but David's response was *alien*!

He was simply watching. He noticed immediately that they were evenly matched and that they were quite paralysed, each with a death grip on the other's clothing, holding each other at bay and therefore unable to move at all. He quietly urged them to keep eyeballing the other to make sure there was no false move and then he spoke:

"Now, I want to see which of you has the greater courage. Keep eyeballing each other and the one who has greater courage, loosen your grip." This approach of unilateral disarmament confused the boys completely, the hostilities subsided into disgruntled mutterings of wounded pride, and the moment was over. David did not punish either boy. The class simply proceeded to the next step.

Like the other incident though, later on a boy approached David and stated, "You didn't break up the fight!?" He was clearly mystified but equally clearly something had happened to him from that experience.

David was not a diplomat and had no particular skills in conflict resolution. His action did not spring from such realms of knowledge at all. In fact David felt chaotic and did not know what to do. However he knew enough to assure himself that acting from such a condition of chaos would surely bring nothing new to the situation. So he waited. He had to wait and take the risk that someone might get hurt and he would surely be blamed. And then he "saw" with objective cognition. He perceived two small boys locked in an embrace, not having the faintest idea what to do next, both subject to forces over which they had no control. They were embracing in rage, and that same rage stormed in David's heart. From the eye of the storm, he acted in accord with his objective cognition. And a new, unexpected outcome was generated. As before, David felt love born in his heart and the rage disappeared or perhaps transformed into that love. The boys had seen nothing quite like it before and simply could not proceed with the usual taunts or rescue attempts.

There was no didactic session afterwards, no post game analysis, nor any moral admonition. The class just moved on.

But with a difference . . .

The days went by and David's work became almost a routine. He no longer experienced antipathy towards the executive branch and neither did he feel polarized into one or another subgroup within the staff relations. His week was long and arduous, often leaving him tired to the point of exhaustion. A dreadful inner conflict had softened to the point of hardly being noticeable and his body began to show signs of recovery from acute and chronic stress. As David brought his attention to the process of bringing love into a loveless context, his misguided attempts "to get out", "find the right form" etc. began to dry up and his inner world responded with dreams. He had a series of dreams where he was approached by figures that embodied love. He was clearly an object of love's desire. He always felt renewed by such inner encounters. In effect David had become self-generative.

There were some strange side effects to this process. All ambition dried up in David. Many times he couldn't think of a reason why he wanted to go anywhere or do anything. In other words his own desires were not focussed on the future: "I want to do this so let's do it . . ."

He felt strangely present through his senses to the world. But was it the same world that others experienced?

He soon learned that it was decidedly not! It was as if David now inhabited two worlds that interpenetrated. The one he shared with others was the usual one of self-consciousness coupled with a world devoid of spirit, merely objects in space. This world was the one that David's old personality belonged to. At the same time he was given occasional glimpses of another world through his new personality. This new personality was participatory with the new world. Thus David could no longer maintain the separations that were child's play for the old personality. When someone was hurt, he felt hurt, not through sympathy but through *identity*.

He perceived people and other forms of being as just that—*forms*, or images, expressive of a deeper meaning that he could objectively cognize sometimes. Sadly he was alone with this world, or so it seemed to him.

He had on occasion attempted to communicate his perceptions to others and was met with blank stares or bewilderment.

On one occasion, he was in the school assembly—an hour long testimony to the deputy headmaster's indefatigable zeal to crush any hint of spontaneity in the boys. On this day the headmaster attempted to show the boys an event out of Jesus' life. He tried to pantomime the parable while the boys, under strict orders, were to "pay attention". The show had all the spontaneity of a Gollum, and fell flat. Apparently the deputy's "search and destroy" mission had not quite weeded out all pockets of resistance and a couple of snickers were heard in the audience. The next moment was priceless for David but sadly it seemed to be a moment he shared with no one else.

The headmaster no doubt had the same paranoid structure as most administrators who achieve a measure of power and therefore inherit the fear of its being undermined from behind, in an act of humiliation. As soon as he got wind of the faint snickers, he wheeled around in a gesture of silent accusation. "Who said that?" was written all over his face. His dank greying hair momentarily swished into his bifocals and blinded him. His tunnel vision glance darted into every dark corner of the auditorium. Fear gripped the assembly. But he was clearly on the losing side in that there was not even a small chance of finding a volunteer for punishment amongst a thousand or so silenced and nervous boys. So, he quickly snapped back, regained his composure and the moment was over.

Except for David who "saw" the whole moment! He leaned over to a colleague and whispered: "Did you notice that? That was a true clown. If only he had brought that force into the pantomime, he would have been a great success." His colleague simply looked blank. And David felt lonely.

It was strange to feel lonely in a world that he knew with utter conviction was possible for everyone. David knew that it was a world that was in the process of being born in and through the human being. Human beings are being drafted into service as co-creators of a new world, forming out of the future and seeking to manifest, transforming the present world.

As the months grew into years, David became more convinced that he had indeed been drafted into service of a new master. It was a service that had taken many years to understand and finally to accept. His old personality had found its correct alignment with the new personality and that alignment was as servant to master.

Something deep relaxed in David over time while he continued his daily tasks at school.

His karmic connection to the Knights Templar was affirmed and he had finally found a way to live his vows of poverty, chastity, and obedience in the context of a modern life. He even found further solace in the rather startling fact that the only school that hired him was one whose stated mission, like the Knights Templar so long ago, was grounded in devotion to the goddess.

The school referred to her as *Mary*!

The Coming Storm

One of the most difficult distinctions to make for the one who is on the spiritual path is that between spirit and one's concept of spirit. Let me explain this a little further: I have an experience of spirit. This comes in the form of living thinking or in picture thinking which, in having the experience, I also think. You could say the spirit thinks its thought out in me as I think that thought. This living thinking is so often strange and unfamiliar to me, in terms of any prior experience of mine. As such, we can say that a possible future is beginning to manifest in me, as I think it out. Now, what happens next? The spirit retires and I am left with a memory of that living thinking. You could say that what I have access to now is reflected thought, i.e., no longer living thought, but thought that can properly be called "mine".

So, what do we have so far? Living thinking happens to me as an incursion of spirit. I participate with this living thinking and so think it out for as long as it lasts; and reflected thought which I can claim and keep as long as I remember it. The former is spirit and the latter is my concept of spirit. It is like having a dream. When we dream we are engaged in an activity that is of spiritual nature but when we wake up we simply have a memory of something that happened last night. We often make the obvious mistake of conflating that memory with the nocturnal activity we participated in.

So here is the problem for the spiritual seeker: Subsequent to a true spiritual experience, we are left with a memory in the form of reflected thoughts or static pictures. We then tend to organize our lives in accord with what we now know about spirit. We stabilize our knowledge into routines and habit. We begin to feel comfortable once more, secure in the knowledge that we are up to date in regards to spirit and its concerns.

Meanwhile spirit has moved on. Unbeknownst to us, even unwanted by us, spirit seeks another incursion into human affairs and does so quite unexpectedly, just when we think we are on top of things. Our precious concepts once again must undergo a melt-down on the way to yet another fresh bout with the living reality of spiritual life.

Get used to it!

Master John: *Perils of the Soul*

Storms often begin softly, with a whisper in the night, like the quiet movement of a butterfly wing. Eight years into David's sojourn as a teacher at the Catholic school, he had a dream:

> *Sigrid returns. I did not think you would come back. So you really do love me then—of course I do. At school, a young woman working in a cafe. We feel intimate. I would have a relationship with you if I were 40 years younger. All through these encounters with younger women I am going over Einstein's theory of relativity, working out the equation. My mind is working it out as I dream within that mind.*

David indeed had had a relationship with Sigrid forty years ago. She was his first love—a love that "married" thinking with the eros/psyche mystery, i.e., soul life. David was Sigrid's maths tutor. He was twenty years old, studying physics and maths at university, and she was fourteen years old, destined to become one of Australia's most beloved actors. Their love, like Dante's love for Beatrice, was not satisfied on the earthly plane, but left an indelible mark in David's heart. She accompanied him for the next forty years, functioning within as his lover, mentor, and initiatrix, while shaping his inner life into visible expression through his writing and other artistic productions.

Her return appearance in David's dream therefore alerted David to a new premonition emerging from the unconscious. The dream was clearly concerned with connecting soul with thinking, as had happened forty years ago but with further refinement on the nature of the thinking that the soul is concerned with. Love and depth are here brought together with an *autonomous thinking* that thinks itself out ("Einstein") through the human being who participates in the thinking by thinking it. David could not help but be reminded of one of his favourite paintings by Caravaggio:

In this work of art, the love flowing between the angelic being and the human being is palpable while, at the same time, he is engaged in thinking the angel's thoughts as they in turn think themselves out through the human on to the page. Following this reflection, David began to feel a little nervous.

Sigrid is my initiatrix. Does this mean I am going to be initiated into a kind of Caravaggio moment? If so who is it that is coming towards me? Who wishes to "enter me, in order to transform himself, long before he happens", as Rilke long ago taught me?

Whenever there is an initiation, there is a death. David knew this truth in his bones and his apprehension grew. Long experience with initiatory processes also had confirmed for David that they always involved the body. The body seems to be the vehicle for the inscription of the spiritual "message" into the spiritual depths of the human being. Ancient practices of scarification were not mere torture—merely hurting the initiate was not the point at all. Rather, scarification is a process of inscription that alters the essential being of the initiate, i.e., his definition. The scars that remain are simply "memory devices" so that subsequently, upon his return to ordinary life, the initiate never forgets his spiritual teaching, i.e., who he has now become, in his essence.

In David's case, he had undergone a spiritual process that involved tremendous heat and his skin bore the brunt of it for over twenty years, leaving its scars along the way. His inner work had been to make conscious discernments from within that heat, i.e., to learn its various inflections, textures, intentions, and intelligences.

Am I in for another round?

David nervously sensed a storm approaching.

Outwardly, in his life as a teacher at the school, matters began to sour. His tolerance for the institution weakened. Each day became more of a chore, less satisfying, more arduous. He began to plan a strategic retreat each day by secluding himself in a classroom during the breaks and lying down on his back on the floor, well out of sight. His ordinary commerce with colleagues dried to a trickle and his engagement with the students was minimal.

I'll just earn my day's pay and be out of there.

It was true. David's sole reason for continuing at the school was now monetary. There was no soul nourishment anymore and David knew enough about himself to sense a dangerous situation. If his soul life was no longer invested in whatever activity he was doing, then to carry on, merely on the basis of his ego needs, was going to raise the psychological stakes considerably.

One day, David noticed a small speck of eczema between his right forefinger and thumb. He unconsciously scratched it off. It returned a little bigger, and another one appeared on the ring finger of his left hand. At the same time, his heat returned, leaving him wasted at the end of a day, and his nightly wanderings between 1 am and 4 am also returned. His face began to glow red to the point that his colleagues noticed it.

Over the weeks his eczema grew and expanded all over his body. His scratching released the herpes simplex virus which deepened the wounds, and then staphylococcus bacteria got in. His wounded skin erupted at an unheard-of level of pain and David entered a nightmarish *nekyia*. Luckily he had accumulated many weeks of sick leave and the new headmaster recommended he take all the time he needed at full pay. It was a priceless gift to David and he accepted.

His days turned into a living hell in which he simply wandered from room to room or lay down, in agony. He was misdiagnosed by several doctors and alternative practitioners and so simply had to endure, wrapping his body in towels to hold the bleeding and weeping skin that would not heal.

Slowly, slowly, over the blurred weeks and then months, David's resistance wore down and his inner world exploded into life. He knew it was coming. He had been warned after all. The dreams he received had a particular emphasis on "physicality" and "death":

> *I lost my job. I am looking for new work as a maths teacher. Surely someone needs me. I am on a motor bike going along a street the wrong way. It is one way the other way. Someone indicates so and I acknowledge. I notice my right leg. It is almost eaten away around the bone which is quite exposed. Flesh is hanging off. It has obviously been this way for some time. Well, there is no going for work now. That is over! I am under a tree and a dog comes, sniffing. He goes for my leg. At first I am alarmed then realize it is only food for him. A horse comes by. Now, some people come. They are from the organisation that assists with the passage across. I am relieved and I start weeping. Memories come and I finally remember my son Chris, I wish he were here but not to be. I lie there quietly. I see a skull. It is mine but how can that be? As I turn it slowly in my hands I marvel at how at one time my brain was in there. Now the time is close I feel my breath going and I ask to be taken under the tree to go quietly.*

And then another dream:

> *I decide to kill myself. A bullet in the head, but it does not kill*
> *me only knocks out brain functions. So now I am alive but in a*
> *very different way. I see Viv, (who killed himself) who tells me*
> *that meningitis is next. I move into a flat in an inner city area,*
> *almost slum where I will become the "Sage of Underwood" or*
> *some such. Kate, the actress from Underbelly sings nearby to me*
> *and the song is beautiful; just beautiful.*

David lay there quietly under the gently swaying willow. He was dying. And he knew it. All resistance was gone now. His exposed brain was thoroughly infected with the bacteria that had rapidly invaded through his nose, once the meninges had broken down.

He could gather himself enough to reflect. After all he had nothing but time on his hands, i.e., until time ran out. He noticed that his dreams had a definite emphasis on the brain and its demise.

And indeed here I am with meningitis, on my last legs.

But he also knew that dreams are self—movements of the objective psyche as reflected so often in the "muddied waters" of the subjective psyche of the dreamer. That is to say, dreams are first and foremost movements of the soul as yet implicit (in the background, the *not yet become*) but determinative in the sense of catching us in those movements as they seek materialization or realization in the world of matter.

So, ever curious, even while he was dying, David began to think.

What is the soul up to in presenting such death imagery while at the same time my body is reflecting those images, in actuality? Here I am dying, alone under this tree with a rotting leg, and a skull, apparently my skull, lies on the grass beside me.

David was familiar enough with the current advances in neuroscience to know that modern consciousness *exists* only as inextricably linked with the brain and the central nervous system. Some researchers go as far as claiming to predict what we think by simply looking at a MRI scan and observing the section of the brain that "lights up"! David's dreams with their focus on the brain's demise could therefore be addressing a soul movement that includes a death of that brain-linked consciousness.

A death must be undergone! And death is final!

Yet both dreams point to a form of existence in which the link between consciousness and the brain is severed. The first dream showed David contemplating his own skull, the skull that once housed his brain. The second dream explicitly described David as being "alive but in a very different way".

David then remembered an article he had read in *TIME* magazine. [87] The issue was devoted to current research exploring the ties consciousness has to the brain with the predominant conclusion that, without the brain, consciousness ceases to exist. The particular article that David remembered was a counter-example to the prevailing wisdom. The author is an orthopaedic surgeon who describes a patient whose brain "had already been destroyed" and yet woke up to say goodbye coherently to his family.

David was next drawn to the disturbing image of meningitis appearing in the dream as an ominous sense of what was to come "next". Meningitis is a disease in which bacteria or virus invades the meninges, the membranes that cover and protect the brain tissue. There are three layers: the *pita mater, arachnoid mater,* and *dura mater*—tender mother, spider mother, and hard mother. David was jolted when he read this description.

My entire brain, my thinking depends on, and is protected by, these three aspects of the mother. This quite ordinary form of thinking, i.e., reflective knowledge is always "of the past" because it is reflective. And this knowledge is thus petrified, frozen, not living. Of course, petrifaction and reflection irresistibly invoke the image of the gorgon, Medusa who like the triune meninges of my dream lies behind all such knowledge and its petrifying effect on living process.

---

[87]   (Mind and Body Special, 2007)

David then fell asleep again and dreamed:

> *Early morning in the city, few people around. Some trams sidle into their station, ready to start the day. I drive into a bay. I will follow them. They start off and as I follow the road gets more and more rocky and narrow. Stones become boulders and all my forward motion is impeded. I get anxious and fearful . . . Then in the city, the broken down part, I see huge cranes lowering a long horizontal piece of stone into place. It is an art work called the "petrified Christ".*

As all movement is constricted, hampered, and finally brought to a halt, with fear reaching the level of terror, the ultimate image is displayed, the petrified Christ.

David then remembered an equally shocking picture that he had received from a friend called, the *New Pieta*.

Carved in fossilized wood (petrifaction), this new Pieta stands in stark
contrast to its predecessors such as Michelangelo's:

David saw straight away that the *New Pieta* shows the mother ineluctably
releasing her son to the grave where we as observers must follow. We are
no longer held by her in pity in kind of suspended condition between life

and death. It is the final release from the mother who no longer seeks to protect, holding death's claim at bay.

Death's claim is now absolute!

And death's claim on me is now absolute!

David's meninges were now no longer protecting his brain-based consciousness and he was being released to his death. The connection between the knowledge gained by this form of consciousness and the mother whose petrifying stare reduces all living processes to stone lingered in David's musings as he lay quietly in his bed of grass, his breath becoming fainter. He began to remember episodes from his own past. He allowed the images to parade before him, as friends might come by for a visit to the departing one. They were also shards, fragments, seemingly no longer held together in a contrived continuity by a self-edifying ego. They came in whatever order, or disorder . . .

As they arrived, first in a trickle, David discovered that he could "ride" one, if he chose, on a basis of attraction or aversion. When that happened, his present state of dying, under the tree where he had been placed, retreated as if receding down a long tunnel and he would *become* the memory, reliving its feeling, its consciousness.

And so he "woke up'" in a class room.

No! You are wrong! You are all wrong! The forces acting on that object sliding down the inclined plane resolve into these partial forces, not those! I'll prove it to you. I am going to send the entire problem to someone at the University of Queensland and we'll see what he says.

Laughter, Mocking!

Einstein!

Dear John, thank you for sending me this problem about mechanical forces. As you can see from my diagram, your construction is not quite right. The forces rather resolve this way when we place the co-ordinate system on the inclined plane . . . yours sincerely, Dr . . . .

Humiliation!

Michael McRobbie! Fat, the butt of many jokes . . . always trying to belong! I don't mock him. I want to be friends. Why doesn't he come over to my place? I always go to his. He wants to be with Wayne Rubenstein, who always rubbishes him, sparing no pains to humiliate him publically . . .

University of Queensland! I love this place. Physics, Maths, conversations, arguments, study!

Michael, I bet you don't know . . .

Well Woodcock all that depends on truth. What is truth, Woodcock?

Silence.

My god, he knows something I do not. He protects himself against the "Rubenstein attacks" with knowledge. He must be studying philosophy. Now I can see how to protect myself against humiliation. I won't be caught off guard again. For starters, I am going to learn a word every day from the dictionary. And, I am going to strengthen my stomach muscles. You can never tell when someone might come at you with a good kick . . .

The shard drifted away and David looked up at the overarching branches of the willow that sheltered him so lovingly in his last moments.

So that is what I was doing—protecting myself for so long with a carefully constructed edifice of knowledge. Protecting myself from what? Humiliation, mockery! At whose hands!? Who stands behind this edifice of knowledge? I have pursued this kind of knowledge for decades, drawing not only from my personal past but the deep past as well.

David then recalled a dream fragment. "You are a Knight Templar", it said. He caught hold of this particular shard and remembered the excitement he had felt when he learned that the vows that the Knight took were: poverty, chastity, and obedience.

These are my vows! How I have lived them during my life!

Swirling memories of being drawn to junk, cast-off clothes, left-over foods, looking for money in the gutters, dreaming of wealth acquired through finding the 1932 penny that was so rare; strangely shy and modest in all things sexual; first girlfriend as late bloomer while at the University of Queensland; eager to obey authority.

Just tell me what to do!

More shards arrived.

Our past goes further back than the 14ᵗʰ century.

David had engaged with the theory of evolution and its geologic time, aligning himself with those who understood evolution as a simultaneous evolution of consciousness and world. He came to understand that present day consciousness was simply an outcome and a transformation of former states of consciousness and their correlative worlds. For example he marvelled at the paintings found in Southern France, over 30 000 years old.

What form of consciousness did we have then?

David could feel the old excitement as he recalled the years of study he had given over to the study of the mutual evolution of consciousness and the world, focussing on what happens to each when a transformation occurs.

Now the memories were losing their grip on him. They gathered around his bed of grass under the old willow tree, but their hold him was now tenuous at best.

He began to realize that these memories were indeed shards. Any meaning they had was an *invested* one.

This must be why we are constantly revising our history texts, our theories of evolution etc. Why, we even revise our personal histories under the influence of therapy or education.

David realized that the meaning-making factor must therefore lie within *us*! When we take up any shard, be it personal history or stretching into geological time, and "find" its meaning, that meaning must have arisen from within us in the first place. So, deep within our almost obsessive preoccupation *with* the past and within the myriad self-serving interpretations *of* the past, must be an impulse to come to know the *being* from which we emerged, in the form of our modern day consciousness. Naturally we first find it appearing outside us as a perception of the world. Usually a culture favours one interpretation or another and this passes as the "truth". But really this kind of truth is nothing more than an official narrative that serves that culture's need to explain its own origin in an extroverted fashion.

Another interesting question arose for David. What happens when an individual arrives at an understanding of this curious "manufacturing" of knowledge of the past? What happens if this individual no longer wishes to favour *any* interpretation of the past.

Let the shards remain shards!

No sooner had these words left David's mouth when a gentle breeze sprung up and began to move the willow branches softly. Like so many leaves, the shards of memories that had gathered around him, as he lay there dying, began to tremble and whirl.

As the late afternoon sun broke through the thick canopy, it seemed to resolve itself into a form. David saw a pair of wings folded forward and eyes that were staring backwards as the light-being, for that surely what it was, began to surge backwards. Its unearthly eyes were fixed on the shards that were gathered there, drawing them together in what became a torrent of glittering light fragments, likewise surging backwards so that angel and shards were moving ever apart, with an increasing velocity, yet the whole scene danced before David's eyes. He heared a dull roar as this catastrophe gained momentum. The angel, moving ever towards the future backwards had its eyes fixed unwaveringly on the shards of the past as its thundering wings beat the torrent into a frothing ever-departing storm wave.

The roar became a cacophany on David's ears and the light gathered in intensity until all he could see was a blinding river of shattered light forms.

And then, David died.

heart still'd
death's will

  terror'd heart
now depart

still'd lake
now awake

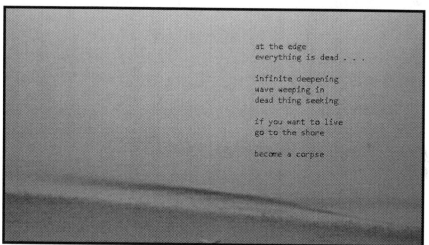

at the edge
everything is dead . . .

infinite deepening
wave weeping in
dead thing seeking

if you want to live
go to the shore

become a corpse

Master John: Death Poems # 3 and #4

Intimations of a New World

Master John sat quietly as people gathered in the large hall. He was a little apprehensive. Expectation filled the air and his childhood asthma niggled at the edges of his mind.

It had happened within a short span of time—only a few years. His memory took him back to "the early days" when his phone never rang, no emails arrived, and he was ignored in conversations.

And he was just John.

One of the reasons he was ignored lay in the fact that he had nothing to say. He certainly perceived a lot—sometimes too much but he had learned over the years that perceiving is one thing, saying another! What John had to say was *expressive* of his perception and so had an impact on others that is quite different from the normal discourse today which is often so self-referential, leading to an endless recycling of what we already know. John almost never knew what he would say next. It just came out and if he suppressed it, he would heat up in his face and throat and break out in a terrible itching that could last for days. So he learned that he must speak when the impulse emerged. He must also take full responsibility for what he said even though he knew inwardly that in a deep sense he was not the author of the speech. These facts led to some very difficult social situations and John grew quieter.

Over time he became familiar with the speech that broke out in him. It seemed that he had only one thing to say and a thousand ways to say it. He was widely read and the concepts he imbibed became vessels for the deeper speech, to be used as needed, often in ways surprising to John afterwards, and to others as well. He was not constructing a coherent ideology as much as finding relevant words "in the moment" that would form a bridge to others. He had even discovered a word for the kind of speaking he was doing—tarning!

All he had to say was, in a nutshell this:

I have found a new world within. It is real. Others have found it also. It is pressing upon us now. It has certain qualities that are verifiable. Other worlds are also pressing upon us, all out of the future. Choices made in our daily lives are co-creating the next world. The one I have discovered, along with others is a world that will manifest through choices made on the basis of love. At present other worlds hostile to humans are manifesting more strongly and these are formed on human choices based in fear. We do not have much time to turn things around.

He knew that current habits of thought are today so entrenched as to exclude such thinking from the outset. After all, he too had been encrusted with these habits until a superior wisdom broke them down and initiated him into new ways of thinking. His task then was to continue speaking what he knew to be true and at the same time gain enough familiarity with current "common sense" perspectives to be able to describe his limitations and blind spots.

So, at first, with other individuals, and then in small groups, John began to speak small utterances, interspersed in the general conversations, like beads dropping on the ground.

You know how Christians believe that Christ's life on earth is THE turning point of history? Well, how come our theory of evolution makes no mention of that fact in its account of history? How do Christian evolutionists deal with that conflict?

Or,

We all agree here tonight that events in the world appear to be pretty chaotic. How come the only response by the major religions of the world is to more loudly proclaim their wisdom? For example, when China raped Tibet, His Holiness said that China taught him to be more Buddhist! But Buddhism was completely impotent to alter this catastrophe. None of the major religions seem to be able to affect what is going on the actual world. And none seem willing to question themselves in terms of their adequacy to deal with the modern world. All the inadequacy it seems to me is laid at the feet of erring humans as always.

Or,

So many spiritual groups founder on the rocks of money or power, as we know. We all agree on that. I can't think of a case where money and power were brought into the spiritual journey as aspects of the dogma, i.e., as aspects of the journey itself, i.e. as spiritual aspects. I don't mean as obstacles to be overcome or resisted, and I don't mean as justifications for materialistic habits, but as teachings that may require some rethinking of the nature of spirit in the world altogether!

John soon learned not to argue the point. Rather, he studied the reactions in people when he spoke in these ways. Mostly there was a pause in the run of conversation and then the hole would close up and it went on as if nothing had been said. Sometimes a widening of eyes occurred momentarily, as if startled or even in fear. Other times a rejoinder would follow as if John sought an argument, which he never did. And so he would resume his silence, offering no resistance, until his antagonist realized he was beating the air. John, in his turn was more often than not musing over his latest utterance:

What does that mean? I didn't know that those two thoughts belong together? They came together in the very act of speaking but what are the implications?

Sometimes it took him years to render the spontaneous insight into understanding.

When John spoke in this way, he sometimes felt others try to assimilate his speech into what they already knew but often they could not do so and the conversation would die. He knew he was speaking out of the future in the sense that something was forming in him at the time of speech. So it could not be assimilated to the past. This made some uncomfortable but John began to perceive that others became curious at times. And something else began to happen! In tiny moments, another person would occasionally turn towards him and engage him. He would be asked to say more.

This led to a difficulty immediately. When John spoke it was a spontaneous utterance, authored deep within his being. He could not access or direct such speech from his ego centre at all. He thus began a frantic scramble to say something that would count as "more". At times the voice would continue and he could relax into it. At other times he simply had to acknowledge that he had no more to say or he would draw upon some previous understanding he had acquired. One thing was certain—he knew the difference between the two forms of speech and had learned to submit to the will of the *other* as it wandered "where men know not".

There were three capacities that John had to develop in relationship to the voice: *poverty, chastity, and obedience.* His "poverty" was a feeling that any knowledge he had acquired over the years paled into insignificance when faced with the wisdom of the voice. He was constantly surprised by the invisible connections that were made in the windswept chaos of his mind, often producing a form of great beauty. He often could not help uttering poetic speech which others began to notice. Of course when asked to "say that again" he could only do so at the cost of its evanescent beauty. It was like seizing a butterfly. There is not much left when you do! He rarely accommodated others in that way. He understood that such requests were often an attempt to seize upon and own beauty.

Furthermore he felt a delicate chastity associated with such speech, one that could be violated easily by invasive questions or demands for more. He felt an obligation to protect such chastity perhaps in the way the Knights Templar would protect a young maiden. Obedience to the voice carried risks at first because a certain degree of surrender to the unknown was required. John never knew what would "come out" when he spoke. If there were some shadowy elements in his personality that were attracted by the occasion, these would sometimes be aired, disturbing the chastity of the maiden speech. Over time, with considerable inner work, this shadow element diminished and John grew more trusting of the voice and more able to surrender to its impulse while remaining aware of his surroundings.

Individuals began to seek him out. He was at a loss what to call the kind of work he was "doing" with these people. Soon, he gave up calling it anything. He also gave up charging any money. He did not know what he was being paid for since what they valued arrived freely.

Just come around and we will talk for an hour or so . . .

And they did! A certain momentum started up and in a relatively short time, John was asked to speak for larger groups and then for a hall full of people on a regular basis. Others began to write his words down and several books were printed and distributed throughout the community.

It seemed to John as if a miracle had occurred. An increasing number of people wanted to hear what he had to say. He had waited for a quarter century for this co-incidence of interests. So many attempts to make a connection, so many misfires that he had almost given up. For so many years he felt the reality of a dream he had so many years ago:

> *I am in a quartet—the four who are to sing the last movement of Beethoven's Ode to Joy. We begin but soon chaos ensues and the quartet is disrupted. The others are singing their parts perfectly. They look at me in astonishment. I am attempting to sing the whole movement myself. I am banished from the orchestra.*

John discovered that he was living a different paradigm. Rather than the whole being broken into parts and then reintegrated, the whole was attempting to express itself through the part. And he was one of those parts. Twenty or so years had to pass before he could understand any of that mystery. In the meantime, he simply endured that "banishment".

Now, his banishment appeared to be ended. John was now even called "Master John". The name began in a small moment. John's wife came home one day from the group they both sometimes attended and casually said that one woman had asked her when Master John was coming back to speak. And so it began. John did not advertise himself that way nor did he encourage such appellations. It just happened along with the growing numbers of people who wanted to come and hear him speak.

He was referred to as Master John! And he began to speak.

Within him, threads of meaning wove together in remarkable speed and complexity. Something emerged each time he spoke, leaving him with much work afterwards, the work of understanding what he had uttered. While he was speaking however, he had a completely different set of concerns. His "effort" went to emptying himself of his own thoughts or images and becoming available to the *other* within to speak through him. He found this process easier as time went on. When the voice "spoke" it was purely an inner "consort with the self" that took place, as his mentor had once told him. The speech said in this sacred space worked its way through ordinary concepts that would be relevant to the questioner or the one who was addressing him. John had once called this process tarning.

John's psychological structure was quite different from and yet a transformation of ancient inspiration. It was like inspiration in that John was the recipient of utterances that were authored outside of his ego. They were unlike inspiration in that John never lost consciousness of his surroundings and so he was able to translate the inner voice into ordinary language for the sake of his listeners. He experienced love as the basis of this process. He loved the voice and felt that he himself was the object of a deep love. He also loved ordinary life and the endless variety of ways that people expressed their individuality to him. Valuing both realms allowed him to form a bridge between the two realms and his talks expressed their underlying unity, which *was* the new world that John felt to be pressing forward into materialization. He now found his greatest joy in co-creating that world with other souls, making it real.

John was even given the word for the social form that he was creating. It came in a dream: *interlocutor.*

What follows is a condensed version of talks given over the course of only a few years. Excerpts may be found in the books Master John left behind when, one day, he mysteriously disappeared, never to be found again . . .

Master John:
It's clear to me we need a new vision of the spiritual life in order to address the material conditions in which we all live and this vision needs to be rooted in a cosmology we can all understand. The material conditions I am talking about include all those symbols that are part of ordinary public discourse: the economy, environment, wars, etc., and the cosmology must be actively related to our current knowledge systems, i.e., physics and mathematics for knowledge of the present, and evolution for knowledge of the past. There is also a great deal of work going into understanding our relationship to the future theoretically as well.

Question:
Are you talking about a new religion?

Master John:
Yes, the new religion is still forming. "Religion" probably is not the best word for the "next", though—it's too encumbered by past meanings! Many individuals are making great contributions to a new meaning. But there are some signs already of how it will be distinctly different from anything we have enjoyed so far. All religions so far are born from genuine spiritual experience which is then codified and taught. Already a separation occurs between direct spiritual experience and concepts that are then taught. This will not happen in the new religion. The direct experience of individuals will have absolute significance and will not be assimilated into a dogma. The way in which an individual expresses the spiritual life is a contribution to the culture, not to be proscribed by regulations. This is the true meaning of freedom which is so important for the transformation of the present world into the new one.

This is a long story but maybe I can say a few things here.

The way in which an individual expresses the spiritual life is simultaneously personal and universal. Many such attempts are garbled but must be tolerated because at bottom we are slowly overcoming the dreadful "Cartesian split" that is dominating modern consciousness. A dual vision is needed and is pressing forward in our psyches. Even in the most subjective statement, a spiritual movement can be discerned with the proper development of certain soul capacities. This development is taking place as an aspect of a new world. It is important that we encourage its development by valuing individual expression over ideologies.

It can get pretty chaotic as we can see in talk shows, staff meetings, and so on—anywhere opinions are sought. We must slow down enough to listen to this cacophony of voices, for within the noise, something is emerging for humankind.

For example you may see me pause before I answer a question. That is because I am resisting the temptation to use your question to segue into an issue I wanted to discuss all along. To do so is a form of psychic incest in which your individual expression is taken over by my own agenda. So many group leaders practice incest in this way. Individuality is swallowed up by ideology. I try instead to feel into your question, to detect the individuality of your question and to respond out of my own individuality. What can come out of that exchange is truly "of the future" and both parties will be surprised.

Another sign of the new "religion", related to the first, maybe even prior to the first, is a sense of love for the other that is born out of our own self-awareness reaching its apogee. A study of the evolution of consciousness shows that we have won a degree of self-awareness, our subjectivity, over centuries. Now it seems to me we have gone as far as we can go in that effort. Our self-consciousness has separated from everything, even our own thoughts, so that we can even change our thinking at will. Philosophy has shown that the final experience of this condition is a kind of nothingness, an abyss that we shrink back from.

But along with our own self-consciousness is an awareness of other self-consciousnesses like us, equal to us in all respects as individual spirits. In effect we have discovered ourselves as a community of individual spiritual beings embodied here on earth.

A concern and love for the other springs from this soil of equality. The new religion will have this form of compassion as the foundation for all moral conduct. This form of compassion is like the old form in that it springs from the heart but it differs from the old in that it is aimed not so much at the ground of being of the person but instead aims at the individual being. Compassion that loves and supports our individuality!

Our new religion will be "without walls". A true catholic religion in which the world itself will be the temple and we will each be stewards! This will be a matter of perception of reality, not an ideology or faith. The new transformed world will be perceived correctly as an expression of divinity in actual experience.

Question:

The transformation of the world! Master John, Don't you mean the transformation of our perceptions of the world? I.e., we learn to see the same world differently?

Master John:

This perhaps the foundational question upon which the fate of humankind and the earth depends. I am not kidding you. This is it. Where we each come down in answering this question will contribute to our transformation or demise. I will try here in this talk to lay out a few of the facts that bring this question into such sharp focus.

Let's take the common sense view first. This is the view that is either stated outright or implied, or assumed as an a priori matter not worth examining as it is so obvious.

This view concerns the solidity of the world we inhabit on a daily basis and experience as a matter of simple and obvious fact. We regard this solidity as obviously being independent of our consciousness. We take this data a step further and make it the unassailable foundation to all our theories of evolution which do not differ on this point. We also project it into the future.

So there it is, an unchanging world (i.e., its solidity being independent of perception), while our perceptions may change and become more accurate. Along with this common sense is the daily experience of space and time that we have today: Mechanical space, empty in itself and containing discrete objects that move in it, and mechanical time that always ticks along independently of us.

Question:

So what's the problem?

Master John:

According to our common sense, this is the world we inhabit and we daily experience this world as independent of our consciousness. It is reality! We therefore base our theories of everything on that reality principle. There IS no problem at all. There are only two circumstances I know of where the reality principle needs to be brought into question: on an individual level, when we encounter experiences whose reality cannot be denied and yet which conflicts with our given reality principle. This is the path to madness or initiation; on a cultural level, if the theories we build on the basis of our reality principle begin to show internal cracks or irreconcilable differences between themselves. When this happens, we typically employ emergency measures such as "specialization" making sure that no discipline converses with any other. And we seek to silence the dissenting voices. If these defensive measures do not work, blood is spilt, the culture transforms, and a new reality principle is born.

I believe we have arrived at this juncture, both individually and culturally. Many individuals today are being opened to experiences that the current reality principle cannot assimilate. We therefore get all sorts of extreme, even wacky, theories coming forward to account for the undeniably genuine experiences. For example there is a plethora of literature addressing the phenomenon of ascension. Our imaginations are gripped by the idea. When our current reality principle tries to account for it, we get literal explanations such as the Hale-Bopp comet theory of the suicidal cult that emerged in California in the 1980's. Others turn to alternative sources of wisdom such as the perennial wisdom and its reality principle of an unchanging ground of being that we emerge from and dissolve back into. Here we find accounts of transformation of consciousness and the body that can achieve ascension. Others commingle reality principles in a rich potpourri of ideas that our culture is awash in today. Many such voices claim final authority and discourse among the voices on a basis of equality seems difficult if not impossible.

I am not adding my own voice to become yet another authority on ascension or any other specific idea. I am an authority on chaos! My own authority rests in my own experiences of chaos and on that basis I can say with certainty that all these theories that are coming forward serve in the very least to proclaim that our present reality principle as I have described it is in trouble, and I would add, terminal trouble. There is no going back to it!

Since you call me Master John then we should discuss what I am master of: I think I can say I have mastered the ability to stay chaotic when necessary and for as long as necessary and I can teach others to do the same. This is a necessary capacity because as someone said, we are now in a cultural crisis comparable to the transition from an Aristotelian "mindscape" to our present cosmology (universe, now) founded on science. And we all know how well that went! The transition between reality principles is chaotic and we would do well to learn how to live creatively in chaos for as long as it lasts.

OK, so much for tonight.

Question:

Master John, you have taught us that this time of chaos is at bottom our reality principle being shaken up on two fronts, the individual and the cultural. What happens to us if we do not take the cue and examine our reality principle and what happens to us if we do?

Master John (sotto voce):

David, it is no wonder I love you. You have a capacity to hold complexity and to let the alchemy stir in the chaos of your own soul until love makes the connections that leap forth in your speech. Sometimes I feel you to be my Ananda or my Govinda.

Master John (aloud):

David, if we choose to examine our current reality principle with all the means available, we will first discover enormous discrepancies among our fields of knowledge. In the time available tonight, I can mention only a few, central examples. Every modern theory of perception holds that the appearance of the world depends on the perceiver. The cornerstone of the field of Phenomenology for example is the concept of intentionality which affirms what I am claiming here. So, when we inquire deeply about what we mean by appearance of the world, we mean the shapes, colours, smells, textures—all those qualities that are considered subjective and beyond the purview of science which only addresses quantities through measurement. In other words, the world of appearances is the world we experience on a daily basis, i.e., the world we each and all inhabit! There is no experiential reason to call this by any name other than the ordinary world in which we live, i.e., the world! That is what I intend to do from now on. The world of appearances is the world in which we live and experience our lives. It is the world.

Now we also have a science of evolution which is comfortable in the notion that our consciousness has changed over the ages. We can put it this way, thanks to the work of anthropologists, mythologists, etymologists and the like: Our consciousness was once far more participatory in nature than it is now. With increasing self-consciousness, this participation in nature began to fade and we began to experience the world "de-spirited" and more as an object "out there" which can be exploited for our own ends, as it is no longer a living other. There is a large general agreement that this is how our consciousness evolved over time.

We also have a science of physical evolution, an evolution of the world. Within this science we conceptualize a world pretty much the same in its essential qualities as the modern world we inhabit now. I described those qualities the other night, particularly the space and time we inhabit now and the solidity of objects with their sharp discreteness in our perceptions.

So, here we have modern theories of perception establishing that the perceiver and the appearance are intimately related and at the same time, quite comfortably side by side, theories of the evolution of our world that rest entirely on a notion of the world as being always as it now appears to our modern consciousness: our consciousness may have evolved but not the world of appearances. The word of solidity and mechanical space and time has always been so and will always be so—according to all our modern theories!

I have already mentioned another irreconcilable collision between theories or positions held today. The conviction that history is meaningful as an image of the eternal unfolding spirit on earth is held dear in one form or another in many religions. Christianity for example stands and falls on the central mystery that a man, one individual, changed the course of history forever. His time on earth transformed the course of history forever by making forgiveness available to all.

At the same time, our accepted theory of evolution never mentions this event. Instead history is considered essentially meaningless, an outcome of random events driven by chance mutation and selection based on adaptations to the environment.

To hold these compartmentalized fields of inquiry up to scrutiny is to perceive cracks in an edifice that can no longer hold itself together. Some have imagined the outcome and I can offer one quote that I happen to remember. This will give you a sense of what could happen, David, in response to the first part of your question:

"Let us nevertheless suppose that the resistances are eventually overcome and try to imagine a second stage of transition. This surely must be a climate of extreme depression amounting in many quarters to despair . . . I am simply forced to envisage an epidemic of something like nervous breakdowns, with probably some suicides, within such solid fortresses of conformity as MIT or the London School of Economics and amongst their alumni."

If we do not attend consciously to our troubled reality principle, and this is the more likely trend I think, then the cracks will continue to widen, and the incongruities will become more obvious. Some will speak up, only to be silenced. Others will see through the bankruptcy of our knowledge systems and turn away from "established authority". We see this happening with our young people even now. A reactive hostility will grow stronger in which no difference in ideas is tolerated but instead is squashed by ever growing sophisticated machinery in public relations.

On the other hand, more and more voices will speak with less and less discernment between opinion, belief, and knowledge. Truth will retire, having no currency in the market place of "anything goes". And we could descend into a real condition of Babel—a kind of incoherence in which language itself loses meaning and what something means to me may mean something different to you, only we no longer can recognize that fact. Dictionaries as carriers of collective meaning may no longer be consulted because, after all, "they are the results of decisions made by a select group in some university and why should their ideas about language be superior to mine".

So, I have given a dark picture of our times and possible outcomes to living today when our own reality principle is being shaken up and we are descending into a state of chaos.

Let's turn to the second part of your question next time.

Question:
Master John it has been some time now since we began to explore the implications of living in a time of chaos, with the reality principle undergoing transformation. I appreciate what you have said and I have meditated on your words for some time. I want to clarify a few things with you. I think I understand that the transformation of the reality principle is inevitable, that such a transformation is not driven by human beings but by evolution, properly understood. And I get that evolution is not properly understood because current theory fails to take into account modern theories of perception that show conclusively the inextricable correlation between consciousness and appearance (which we know is the real world).

My question is: what follows if we do hold that connection firmly in our minds at all times and not abandon it when we examine our own past, both recent and ancient. And what implications can we draw for our collective future? Do you perceive as dark a picture for us?

Master John (sotto voce):
David my time is drawing near. I sense it and I sense equally that your time is coming. The synchrony of our lives, yours and mine, will become clear to you very soon now. For now, I will address your questions with all the love I feel for you but I must also hold a secret in my heart. You will come to know of it soon. You still feel me as other, as outside yourself, with some wisdom that you are drawn to, like a moth. Remember my David what happens to the moth!

*We may seek the light of wisdom but the fire of love finds **us**!*

Master John (aloud):
Our current theory of evolution and cosmology speak of a universe and world that are independent of our perceptions, as I have said. The central consequence of this habit of thought is that we inhabit a world that is

meaningless. We are developing more and more theories within different disciplines to support this feeling. At the same time, we teach our children from a very early age that our acute self-awareness is an organ of choice and freedom. We can choose anything at all, in freedom.

No wonder we live in an age of anxiety with a proliferation of mental illness. Who can live in sanity, knowing that you can choose anything at all while living in a world where no choice really matters in the big picture, where it is all meaningless? This is a prescription for despair, for breakdown. Yet the refusal to shake up that picture is hardening and is resistive to the most compelling evidence to the contrary. If I may give one stunning example before I turn to your question more fully, David:

We are told in no uncertain terms that our world, Earth is but one speck among countless specks; that it emerged in its present state over an unimaginable stretch of time during which random events occurred finally producing life and then at the very end, consciousness. To be on Earth has no special meaning at all. There is no doubt, we are told, that other planets like ours are somewhere, supporting some kind of life. In no way are we to hold ourselves as special in any way.

This dismal picture flies in the face of overpowering evidence to the contrary—evidence gleaned from science itself and denied by science to be evidence to anything contrary. For example, when we rocketed into space, looked back on Earth and took those first photos, did we not all perceive for ourselves, that precious blue jewel hanging in the blackness of space? Is there anything remotely like it for the eye to see anywhere else? Nothing! Yet we persist in saying: Nothing special here! We have spent millions, billions, of dollars searching for life on Mars and beyond. Has any been discovered? Yet we keep looking, supported by tax payers' money. We build radar telescopes to scan deep space for signs of intelligence, again at huge costs, even though we know that the chances of communicating with other forms of life are infinitesimal with this means. Yet we keep asserting: Life must exist elsewhere!

We override our perceptions and other evidence with a habit of thought that has become our cosmology. I don't think I have ever seen such a hardening of thought in the face overwhelming evidence to the contrary!

What is at stake here?

If for a moment we accepted that nothing found by science has given us a scintilla of encouragement to continue spending billions in order to verify the "non-special" status of Earth in the universe, then we would be left with what our own science screams at us: We ARE in a special corner of the universe, where Earth is tilted just right to support seasonal life, our magnetic field is just right to divert harmful rays from the sun, and so on and on, miracle after miracle.

Having discovered what it takes to support life here on Earth, and having found not one jot of evidence that such support exists elsewhere in the universe, we refuse the obvious reasonable conclusion from the weight of evidence and continue the ever hardening habit of thought that is killing us all: Earth is nothing special and nor are we.

To overcome this habit of thought is to offer a fatal challenge to our cosmology and theory of evolution. This is what is at stake. Instead we would be faced with a universe that holds meaning! We would have to rethink our origins, our past, and our present, and many careers and lives would be lost.

David, this is a compelling example of what is at stake when we choose to hold in thought what we already know: that the world of appearance (i.e. our world) and our consciousness are correlative and we cannot discuss the evolution of one without at the same time discussing the evolution of the other. Our reality principle must dissolve and we must fall into chaos, until such time as a new reality principle emerges, one that is more embracing and less fragmented in terms of the fields of knowledge that we have developed so far today. At present our habit of thought is producing incoherence in our disciplines of knowledge and the only protection we have is to isolate disciplines from one another. This is not sustainable.

Far better for us to enter the chaos and to hold what we know to be true in consciousness as we seek understanding of our collective past, present, and future. Where is the hope? Right in the middle of the despair—if we can enter it consciously! This means a descent into the maelstrom for us all and we have to learn how to do this, how to live this way, for as long as it takes. Tomorrow night I will take you there, just a little way into the maelstrom and we will see what we can discover together.

Question:
You said last night the world of appearances is not independent of our consciousness and yet our common sense shouts it out to us. How are we to overcome that to come into accord with our modern theories of perception that affirm what you say, Master John?

Master John:
Yes, a good place to start tonight! OK! Let's start with how a hardened habit of thought is challenged. There are two aspects. As I said a reality principle only needs to be examined when individuals have experiences that can no longer be "held" in the reality principle or when the reality principle can no longer assimilate a growing body of data emerging from the culture. These things have happened. We have arrived at that point. But as you perhaps could see from my example of our Earth's being special or not, the habit of thought can harden even more against such evidence. Even though many authors express in theory the possibility of other reality principles, if you read between the lines, you find they have not really given up their common sense which you described well in your question. So, we get distorted arguments such as "the world of solid objects in empty space and mechanical time has existed for ever and it is only our perceptions of that world that have improved and become more accurate over time. Our ancestors were simply mistaken in what they perceived of the world."

So, as you can understand, habits of thought are not overcome by argument, or evidence provided by others. Our common sense view of ourselves and the world, i.e., the view that we are born into during this time can only be overcome by a compelling experience of another reality principle that cannot be reduced to the present one. Therefore there is a two-pronged approach to this:

It has been always the case that when the reality principle is undergoing transformation, certain individuals are "called" to experience that transformation within their being. I myself was one. This fact alone does not make me special—although I had my moments of feeling special. But they only last as long as you haven't grasped the responsibility that comes with the gift. The only qualification needed to become a candidate to experience the reality principle undergoing a transformation is to be wounded in your personality so that there is a hole through which spiritual influences may enter. This fact is also testimony to the way in which we have developed personalities that keep the spirit from entering, in our western culture. It takes a wound, a trauma, to undo that hardened personality. I must have been particularly obdurate because my experiences were a little rough on me.

At present such individuals are going through their dark night of the soul, alone and with much misunderstanding on the part of others. They must be allowed to go through these experiences the right way and that way as I have said is to develop some tools with which one can enter chaos consciously, for as long as it takes, until something emerges from that chaos.

Secondly, what we can do culturally is develop teachable capacities that attune us to the realities that initiates are discovering through direct experience. We can learn how to listen to individual voices in their own terms. We can learn to give up the pernicious habit of translating whatever anyone else says into terms that we already know, thinking thereby that we understood what they have just said. We haven't! We can allow other individuals to influence us instead of forever seeking to reaffirm ourselves in terms of the known past. All these and other capacities are teachable and our education system needs to emphasize them.

Initiates perceive a new reality principle through direct experience. They can then teach others to perceive the same reality by means of extending the meanings of our concepts. This has always been so and is the proper function of teaching. Spend a little time in the mountains with a geologist explaining his concepts to you and pretty soon you will be perceiving a whole new appearance, one that is real but only seen by geologists. More and more people are directly experiencing a transformation in our reality principle itself. They will become our new teachers and we must let them do so, no matter how weird they sound or look. We must let ourselves be taught by them and with their help we will as a culture perceive a new reality too.

Then a collision of habit of thought and direct perception will take place and we need to support the new and gracefully surrender the old in favour of the new. It won't be easy but it offers much hope.

So, this much for tonight . . .

Unity of Difference

David, David, Wake up!

What? What? What's going on?

Wake up!

Where am I? I can't move!

C'mon David. Wake up! You know where you are. You've been here many times. You know the territory well.

Who are you! Master John, is that you? Why can't I move?

O dear, you can't have forgotten. Relax. You don't have to breathe here. Your body is just fine. Don't fight it. You are here with me. I found my way to you at last. It took some work mind you. You are not the clearest light around you know. But the green around your heart is strong and vibrant and pulled me towards you. And David, some blue is growing stronger in the Cave of Brahma, can you feel it? At last, I have found you and my work is near the end.

OK! OK! Relax! Where am I? Master John, Master John where are you? I feel you here but cannot see you. What do you mean your work is almost done?

I didn't know halls could be this huge. My heavens! What a crowd. Such a feeling of anticipation! Everyone is thronging towards that door. Someone is coming. This feels so familiar. O my God, it's Master John coming through the door. O the love the love. It's almost too much. How can one Being hold that much love? I feel so . . . small. I want him to see me but he may not and I am content to see him. So many clamour for his attention and he sleights no one! His eyes meet mine. I drink in the love. Pools of emptiness! Momentary terror, now love flows through into me. I am filled with love. Compassion flows through emptiness. He has just given me a mantra. My prayer is answered yet there is more. How can I take more? Master John, how is it that you are here in front of me? No answer, I do not need an answer. Your presence is the answer—the answer to all my questions. I am ready. For what?!

It doesn't matter. I am ready.

As I am, my beloved David.

Where has the crowd gone? Where are we now?

Where we have always been David, you and I. We!

Aah! I feel you. O the Light, the blinding light! No! Filling light, life-giving light! Light is all. Enter me, I enter you. Let me vanish in you.

I and you are one.

My work now here

Is done.

Epilogue

There were many loose ends but that is in accord with a life fully lived. When women of traditional societies wove their rich tapestries or carpets, they would customarily leave a loose thread at the end. Life does not end. It continues and new patterns are woven, ceaselessly.

At first there was great consternation. No one could find him. Master John had apparently disappeared without a trace. The usual jealousies sprung up as various people realized they were not the ultimate confidante that they had imagined themselves to be. A brief excursion into paranoia followed and dark conspiracies were hatched and quickly aborted. His room was as he left it. There was no sign of violence or even disturbance, when I and others visited it. No one was even sure when he was seen last. No one that is, except me. I knew and I wasn't telling anyone. Not because of some sense of being the owner of a precious secret. I just couldn't find a way to say it. Language failed until now, some years later, I am able to tell, at least a little of what happened.

It was only recently that I felt a loosening of my tongue and a flowing start up in my fingers. I began to write without knowing what I was writing. It just came and I recorded what came, just as I am doing now. I suppose an embargo has been lifted according to some mystery of timing that I still have yet to understand. No matter, I am writing and I have my favourite painting on my desk as I write.

Guido Reni's *Saint Matthew and the Angel* looks up at me and I see Matthew accepting the inspiration of the love being who whispers wisdom, while gazing deeply into his eyes, commanding Matthew's rapt attention, which he gives freely.

His hand records their encounter.

I too follow the invisible command of my master.

After a time conspiracy gave way to conjecture and then a release of imagination which opened up fruitful pathways in the new culture dawning in the West. But even more mysterious events followed. Master

John had left a huge legacy of writing, much transcribed from his talks, that he freely gave to groups for the few short years he was with us (how strange to put it that way. I do not feel him missing at all). His book titles are listed but the publishing houses are not. Were they ever listed? No one seems to quite remember. We also remember many talks, going on for hours, but all that I can recall is recorded here in this testimony. There was so much more but all efforts to find it, or even recall it have failed. For the sake of his memory I have recorded a bibliography of Master John's works but it is very incomplete and I do not think any further research along those lines will yield any more knowledge. But the mystery will surely deepen.

Master John is a master of chaos and I suppose these incomplete fragments of his work are fitting flotsam and jetsam. Make of it what you will. It is the best I can do.

What is left for me? Well, I look forward to the next day. I will go to work at my desk and I will do a good job. I will practice my daily discipline of living in the chaos. I benefit from everything Master John has taught me about chaos and how to live in it, how to synchronize with it—for as long as it lasts, until it ends, when the child of chaos springs forth from it, making new connections and bringing love into a world that is starving for love.

I, David, or is it John? I can't seem to remember the difference. O well, let's stick with John since that is what I began with. I, John leave this book with you, my reader, with love and hope for the future. Take it into the chaos with you. Let it be a companion for you, perhaps even a source of courage, to help you stay in the chaos, as long as it lasts, until the child of chaos leads you into the future that evolution has intended all along, for you, for all of us.

Welcome!

Bibliography (incomplete)

Master John Speaks: *Lesson I: Introduction to the Spiritual Problem of Our Times*

Master John: *Aphorisms*

Master John: *Death Poems*

Master John: *State of our Modern Psychology*

Master John Speaks: *Lesson IV: Intimations of the Future*

Master John Speaks: *Lesson VII: Perils of the Soul*

Master John Speaks: *Lesson X: The Manifestation Process*

Master John: *Commentaries*

Master John Speaks: *Questions and Answers*

Master John: *Lecture Series on Service*

AFTERWORD

J: Grandfather, can you hear me?

SJ: One minute, lad, I just have to untangle this skein—there, done! Sorry, lad, a customer came in tomorrow, and thanked me for the dress I made for her, before I started it. I didn't know what to say to her, so I thanked her for paying promptly, but then, to make matters worse, she asked me for the bill. That's the last time I leap off that cot before the bell rings—or is it the first? After? O dear!

J: Is it too soon for us to meet again, Grandfather? I can wait.

SJ: Not at all, my boy. And I see you have sharpened your own shears. I knew you were coming when I smelled the pungency—slipped a stitch in the process. No matter! Well, I am happy for you, very happy. You are finally ready to begin your own business. I can see that! Do you have everything you need—thread, needle, of course your shears, and you still have that army-knife set I sent you, I hope. Or am I about to send it? Remember nobody is to touch those shears. You never know where you may end up, or begin.

J: Grandfather, I finished the garment. Would you like to see it?

SJ: Oh, I will see it when it is done, lad. Remember, I will tell you that his name is to be "David".

J: Why "David", Grandfather?

SJ: My beloved Grandson, can you not foretell? After all, what are yours and my *given* names? Now let me give you one more piece of advice, an extra button to stitch into your garment, just in case. Language is the garment. You must use the seam ripper carefully to avoid cutting the threads. We unravel, we don't destroy. Loosen only! Alter the pattern subtly. Syntax only! That's how you move about. Ask yourself, "When am I?" not "Where am I?" You alter space by closing the thread. The *uroborus*, lad, you know that, the snake! We get there by already always having been there! Just as you are with me now! You call me Grandfather; I call you my beloved Grandson, yes? Yet how could come to me now without already having been here. So, I say to you, Grandfather, thank you for coming to me now and showing me how to sew this garment which you will never see, that you wanted me to do *for* you, for *us*.

J: Keep your shears with you at all times . . .

WORKS CITED

(2012, 12 5). Retrieved from Hearing Voices Network: http://www. hearing-voices.org/

Baljeu, J. (2012). *Downloading Spirit.* www.xlibris.com.au: Xlibris.

Barfield, O. (1957). *Saving the Appearances: A Study in Idolatry.* London: Faber and Faber.

_____. (1967). *Speaker's Meaning.* Rudolph Steiner Press.

_____ (1977). *The Rediscovery of Meaning.* San Rafael : Owen Barfield Press.

Bernays, E. L. (1928). *Propaganda.* New York: Horace Liveright.

_____ (1965). *Biography of an Idea: Memoirs of a Public relations Counsel.* New York: Simon and Schuster.

Carroll, L. (2012, 11 25). *Jabberwocky.* Retrieved from Lenny's Alice in Wonderland site: http://www.alice-in-wonderland.net/jabberwocky. html

de Cervantes, M. (1997). *Don Quixote.* (J. Ormsby, Trans.) Project Gutenberg. Retrieved 11 23, 2012, from http://archive.org/stream/ donquixote00996gut/old/1donq10.txt

Freud, S. (1961). *Civilization and its Discontents.* (J. Strachey, Ed., & J. Strachey, Trans.) New York: Norton.

Gatto, J. T. (2012, 11 27). *Chapter 16: A Conspiracy Against Ourselves.* Retrieved from The Odysseus Group: John Taylor Gatto: http://www. johntaylorgatto.com/chapters/16c.htm

Giegerich, W. (2001). *The Soul's Logical Life.* Frankfurt: Peter Lang.

_____ (2003, December 2). *The End of Meaning and the Birth of Man.* Retrieved December 13, 2010, from http://www.cgjungpage. org/index.php?option=content&task=view&id=332

_____ (2004). After Shamdasani. *Spring 71*, 193-213.

_____ (2007a). Psychology as Anti-Philosophy: C. G. Jung. *Spring 77*, 11-53.

_____ (2007b). *Collected English Papers Volume II: Technology and the Soul.* New Orleans: Spring Journal Books.

_____ (2010). Liber Novis, that is, The New Bible, A First Analysis of C. G. Jung's Red Book. *Spring 83*, 361-413.

_____ (2012, 11 7). *The Flight into the Unconscious: A psychological analysis of C. G. Jung's psychology project.* Retrieved from Rubedo: http://www.rubedo.psc.br/artingle/flight.htm

Giegerich, W., Miller, D. L., & Mogenson, G. (2005). *Dialectics and Analytical Psychology: The El Capitan Canyon Seminar.* New Orleans: Spring Journal, Inc.

Gleick, J. (1997). *Chaos: The Amazing Science of the Unpredictable.* London: Vintage.

Hillman, J. (1981). *Eranos Lectures 2: The Thought of the Heart.* Dallas: Spring Publications.

Hornstein, G. A. (2009). *Agness Jacket: A Psychologists Search for the Meanings of Madness.* New York: Rodale, Inc.

Intervoice. (2012, 12 5). Retrieved from http://www.intervoiceonline.org

Jung, C. G. (1963). *Memories, Dreams, Reflections.* New York: Random House.

_____ (1975). *C. G. Jung Letters* (Vols. 2 (1951-1960)). (G. a. Adler, Ed., & R. F. Hull, Trans.) London: Routledge and Kegan Paul.

_____ (1989). *Analytical Psychology: Notes on the seminar given in 1925.* (W. McGuire, Ed.) Princeton: Princeton University Press.

_____ (2009). *The Red Book.* (S. Shamdasani, Ed., S. Shamdasani, M. Kyburz, & J. Peck, Trans.) New York: W.W. and Norton & Company.

Kingsley, P. (2001). *In the Dark Places of Wisdom.* London: Duckworth.

Lewis, C. S. (1943). *Perelandra.* London: Harper Collins.

_____ (2012, 11 29). *C. S. Lewis Lectures on the Novels of Charles Williams.* Retrieved from YouTube: https://www.youtube.com/watch?v=Z5w134gYz04

Lockhart, R. A. (1987). *Psyche Speaks: A Jungian Approach to Self and World.* Wilmette: Chiron.

Marlowe, S. (1996). *The Lighthouse at the End of the World.* New York: Plume.

Mind and Body Special. (2007, 1 29). *Time.*

Rayner, A. (2010). *NatureScope.* Hants: John Hunt Publishing.

Rilke, R. M. (1939). *Duino Elegies.* (J. B. Leishman, Trans.) New York: W. W. Norton & Co.

_____ (1996). *Rilke's Book of Hours: Love Poems to God.* (A. a. Barrows, Trans.) New York: Riverhead Books.

Shamdasani, S. (2003). *Jung and the Making of Modern Psychology.* Cambridge: Cambridge University Press.

Smith, T. (2011). *Contemporary Art: World Currents.* London: Laurence King Publishing.

Sugerman, S. (Ed.). (1976). *Evolution of Consciousness: Studies in Polarity.* Middletown: Wesleyan Uiversity Press.

Tacey, D. (2010). Ecopsychology and the Sacred: The Psychological Basis of the Environmental Crisis. *Spring 83*, 329-353.

Tarnas, R. (1991). *The Passion of the Western Mind: Understanding the Ideas That Have Shaped Our World.* Reading: Cox and Wyman Ltd.

Tillyard, E. (1942). *The Elizabethan World Picture: A Study of the Idea of Order in the age of Shakespeare, Donne & Milton.* New York: Vintage Books.

Tolstoy, N. (1989). *The Coming of the King.* New York: Bantam Books.

Williams, C. (2003). *The Place of the Lion.* Vancouver: Regent College Publishing.

ABOUT THE AUTHOR

John C. Woodcock holds a doctorate in Consciousness Studies (1999). His thesis articulates the process and outcome of a spiritual ordeal that lasted twenty years. At first it seemed to John that he was undergoing a purely personal psychological crisis but over time, with assistance from his various mentors, he discovered that he was also participating in the historical process of a transformation of the soul as reflected in the enormous changes occurring in our culture, often referred to as apocalyptic. During this difficult period of John's life, he wrote two books: *Living in Uncertainty* and *Making of a Man*. Both books have been expanded into second editions (2012).

Over time John began to comprehend how empirical or Cartesian reality, seemingly so bereft of soul, is indeed itself a manifestation of soul. Soul and world were found to be a unity of differences. This discovery opened up the possibility of discerning soul movement from within present external reality, comprising hints of the unknown future. John's next three books, *The Coming Guest*, *The Imperative*, and *Hearing Voices*, explore this idea more fully by describing the initiatory process and outcome of a human being's becoming a vehicle for the expression of the unknown future, through the medium of his or her art. John's latest book, *Animal Soul*, establishes a firm theoretical ground for the claim that the soul is urging us towards the development of new inner capacities that together he calls the augur-artist mind—the mind that can discern and artistically render hints of possible futures. In this new book John gives a more refined definition of the genre of literature that can adequately express/describe a new reality that is forming in the unconscious—one that overcomes the oppositions that characterize the Cartesian reality principle.

John currently lives with his wife Anita in Sydney, where he teaches, writes, and consults with others concerning their soul life. He is also a practicing Jungian therapist.

He may be contacted at *jwoodcock@lighthousedownunder.com.*